THE COURSE BEAUTIFUL

A Collection of Original Articles and Photographs on Golf Course Design

By Albert Warren Tillinghast
The Dean of American Born Golf Course Architects

[signature]

Compiled, Designed and Edited by
Richard C. Wolffe, Jr. and Robert S. Trebus

Library and Pictorial Research by Stuart F. Wolffe

Dedicated to Albert Warren Tillinghast

Gratitude to our faithful wives, Liz and Dee, and our children, Rachel, Matthew, Tami, and Christopher for all their support.

We would like to acknowledge the many Tillinghast Clubs, the people from those clubs and many others from the golf world for their many contributions. This book would not have been possible without them: Dr. Glenn Alexander, David Applegate, Dr. Philip W. Brown, Jr., Mike Chernack, Warren Chancellor, Louis Chanin, Susan Cummings, Gregory R. Davis, Mark DeNoble, Bob Denny, Marge Dewey, Alan Easter, Pamela Emory, Joe Flaherty, Maynard Garrison, Stephen Goodwin, Tom Hand, Bruce Hepner, Phil Hodges, Red Hoffman, Tom Hurst, Tom Jarzyna, Rees Jones, Mike King, Brad Klien, Pete Korba, Joe Martone, Bob McCoy, Dan McKean, Randy McKelvey, Terry McSweeney, F. Duffield Meyercord, Bob Miller, Scott Musmanno, Laura Puchaiski, Bob Ross, Saundra Sheffer, Lowell Schmidt, Douglas L. Smith, Ken Stofer, Craig Surdy, Rayburn Tucker, Jim Smith, Nancy Stulack, Hugh Vahn, Ron Whitten, Benita Wolffe. For those we have accidentally omitted, we offer our deepest apologies.

We also express our deepest thanks to:
1. The Library and Museum of the United States Golf Association and the Library of Congress of the United States for the courtesy of allowing the reproduction of many of the photographs.
2. The PGA of America for the courtesy to reprint specific Tillinghast articles and sketches which were originally published in the *Professional Golfer of America.*
3. Baltusrol Golf Club for permission to reprint and edit "The Creator of Baltusrol" by Stephen Goodwin from *Baltusrol 100 Years*.

Library of Congress Catalogue Card Number: 96-090222
ISBN 0-9651818-0-4

Printed in the USA by Progress Printing, Lynchburg, VA

FOREWORD

GOLF is a game in which the player's true opponent is the golf course. That is why the game can be enjoyed in solitude or with other golfers of every caliber and age. Few golf books have been published that help the recreational golfer understand the playing ground, its challenges and its variety. *The Course Beautiful,* the writings of architect Albert Warren Tillinghast, is such a book. Each chapter covers a different aspect of golf course design.

A.W. Tillinghast was totally immersed in the game of golf as a player, writer and architect in the early decades of the twentieth century. He loved the game and he understood its nuances so well that his knowledge and insights enabled him to build some truly remarkable golf courses. Those of us who are fortunate enough to continually play his courses never tire of his designs. *The Course Beautiful* gives us insights as to why his designs have stood the test of time. Most of his design principles are still in vogue today. In fact, the golf architecture of the 1990's in many cases is a throwback to the styles and principles of the designs prior to the Great Depression of 1929.

Tillinghast was the renaissance man of golf in that he played the game well, conceived design ideas, wrote about them, transferred these ideas to his design plans and implemented them in person on the construction site. Because he was an accomplished student of the game his courses not only have endured, but have endured with minimal revision.

I think every Tillinghast course is a work of art, mainly because Tillinghast built the golf courses he designed. He oversaw the day-to-day construction and personally directed the shapers to make sure they built the greens in the manner in which he designed. He didn't go out and pound 18 stakes on the course on a Sunday afternoon and leave.

Golf course design has always been a very competitive business. Everyone talks about the numbers. If you mass produce, it's difficult to continually produce quality. If it's an original or a limited edition it's thought to be better. Tillinghast built limited editions that emulate nature. He did not force artificial features on a course. In total he built around 70 original courses and redesigned or remodeled about 70 more—personally instilling quality into every one of them.

Reading this book will help all golfers understand the concepts, style, nuances and subtleties of one of America's great golf course architects. Discovering the design ideas of A.W. Tillinghast through his writings will deepen your appreciation of the courses you play.

Rees Jones
Montclair, New Jersey

TABLE OF CONTENTS

THE CREATOR OF GOLF COURSES

ALBERT WARREN TILLINGHAST cut a commanding figure in American golf during the first third of this century. Born in 1874, he took up the game with a passion early in life and, to put it simply, became a fixture on the golf scene. He seemed to be on hand for every major event and to know everyone who mattered. He was friend to Old Tom Morris and many of the other "old timers" of golf such as Andra Kirkaldy and Old Daw. Remembering Old Tom, Tillinghast wrote:

Playing around the Old Course at St. Andrews with the patriarch made me feel as though my own game must seem glaringly new, just like walking up the church isle in new, squeeky boots, but this feeling soon vanished. The old man and I were just boys together, for such is golf and such was "Old Tom Morris."

Indeed, there was hardly any facet of the game that Tillinghast did not explore. Any full account of his life would have to include a multitude of scenes in which Tillie, as he was known in the golf world, appeared in different roles. Tillie the photographer carried the best camera equipment on his pilgrimages to Scotland, where he took superb pictures of golf scenes and celebrities. Tillie the author wrote humorous, fictional pieces about golf which his daughter, Elsie, would later describe as "immense, gushing sentimentalism." Tillie the advocate was forever promoting the virtues of public golf, and Tillie the entrepreneur owned a combination miniature golf course-driving range with lights, covered booths, and long-hitting contests. Tillie the phrase maker is said to have coined the word "birdie," though by his own account the term came into more or less spontaneous use among a group of Philadelphia golfers of which he was a member.

Tillie the tournament organizer ran the Shawnee Open, and Tillie the statesman was one of the founders of the

PGA of America. Tillie the reporter wrote a syndicated column and published annual, highly subjective, and eagerly awaited rankings of the top 12 Americans in three categories—professional, amateur, and woman amateur (in 1916, after his first sight of Bobby Jones, Tillie had the foresight to name the 14 year old as the No. 12 Amateur).

Tillie the player had enough of a game to make a respectable match against the top amateurs of the day, though never quite enough to beat them on the big occasions. Tillie the green keeper was the champion of the fledgling USGA Green Section and its agronomic turf research.

The mere listing of his activities suggests, correctly, a man of enormous energy and gusto. He also had a volatile and flamboyant personality. The spoiled son of a wealthy Philadelphian, Tillinghast grew up doing exactly as he pleased and never finished a single school he attended. Like many other men of his class and time, he was a prodigiously heavy drinker, and the Tillinghast legend contains accounts of long binges, epic parties, lavish spending, and pistol-flourishing rages. He was a spellbinding talker, a flashy dresser, and a good hand at the piano. His trademark was a magnificent waxed mustache. With his wife and two daughters he lived in a splendid columned house in Harrington Park, New Jersey. In a word, Tillinghast was the embodiment of the sporting gentleman of the Roaring Twenties.

Yet Tillinghast would merit nothing more than an honorable footnote in golf history had he not become a golf course architect. His first commission came in the form of an invitation from a wealthy friend to lay out Shawnee-on-the-Delaware in 1909. At the time Tillinghast was 34 years old, and hardly seemed to have the temperament or discipline for any sustained enterprise. But he threw himself into the task and produced a course that was instantly hailed as a success. Tillinghast was on his way. For the next three decades he lived and breathed golf architecture.

The enduring image of Tillinghast is that of the architect, always impeccably dressed and groomed, poring over the plans for a golf course. He was very much a hands-on architect who liked to make his designs "in the dirt," relying on the inspiration of the moment to fashion the details of each hole as it emerged from the landscape. In the accounts passed along by old-timers, Tillinghast's working method was to seat himself in the shade of a tree, bottle in hand, and call out directions to his workmen as they shaped the course with their mule-pulled scoops. As golf historian Herb Graffis wrote, "The laborer

Many of Tillinghast's design principles were shaped in Scotland in the early 1900's. Here young Tillinghast prepares to drive on the links at St. Andrews' Old Course in 1898.

and mule would occasionally get a sniff of Tillie's richly-flavored exhaust and knew they were working for a man of great power and artistry."

In 1918, when Baltusrol Golf Club in Springfield, NJ hired him to construct a second course, Tillinghast was just hitting his stride. His services as an architect had been in demand, but his golf courses were spread across the continent—Atlantic in Florida, Brackenridge in Texas, and San Francisco in California. In New Jersey, he had built the Shackamaxon and Somerset Hills courses, but he had never won a commission of the magnitude and prestige of Baltusrol. For Baltusrol was already in the vanguard and its "old course" had hosted two U.S. Opens, three other USGA national championships, and several other national tournaments. Strictly speaking, no American golf architect before or since has ever received such a commission, and Tillinghast stood to gain more from Baltusrol than

Baltusrol stood to gain from Tillinghast.

Instead of simply building the second course, Tillinghast boldly recommended that the "Old Course" be plowed over to make room for two new courses. As it turned out, both Baltusrol and Tillinghast were winners. For Tillinghast's work at Baltusrol – The Upper and Lower courses – placed him securely in the first rank of American golf architects. Throughout the 1920's he was a whirlwind of activity, building or remodeling golf courses all over the country. Some of his more notable courses included Winged Foot, Ridgewood, Quaker Ridge, Five Farms East, Newport and the Bethpage Black. His career lasted until the Great Depression brought golf course construction to a standstill, but Tillinghast managed to stay in the game as a course inspector for the PGA. When that job ended, he went west to California. There he went into a golf course architecture partnership with Billy Bell while his wife opened an antique shop where they seem to have sold off many of the possessions they had collected over the years. In 1940, after a heart attack, he went to live in Toledo, Ohio, with his eldest daughter, Marian. He died there in 1942.

For several decades he was forgotten by the golf world, though his courses continued to give pleasure and to serve as tournament sites. In recent years the extent of his legacy to American golf has come to be better understood and appreciated, for it is abundantly clear that Tillinghast had a genius for building golf courses that endure. In retrospect it seems that he deserved all along the title he gave himself— the "Creator of Golf Courses."

Young Tillinghast at the turn at St. Andrews. "Auld" Da dispensed ginger beer, bisquets and golf balls from a perambulator.

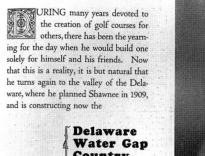

REMEMBRANCES OF MY GRANDFATHER

There is no great genius without some touch of madness.
— Seneca, circa 50 A.D.

This saying applies well to my Grandfather, Albert Warren Tillinghast. My sisters and I knew him as Dadgan, probably a youngster's corruption of "Grand Dad." Many of the stories that follow were provided by our mother, Elsie Tillinghast, who was Dadgan's younger daughter. Other recollections are from my two sisters, Pam and Fran and my cousin, Bobby Jane, who was born to Dagdan's older daughter, Marion. A few months prior to her death in 1974, mother came up with extensive recollections of Dadgan at the request of Frank Hannigan, who at the time was an Executive of the USGA. Hannigan used much of this material in his 1974 article in *Golf Journal*. I mention this only so you will understand that I relate material from about as direct a source as I know. But I recognize that the matter may be tainted by mother's memory faults at that time, and by those of mine at the present.

Born in 1874, Tillie—Bertie—A.W.—Dadgan—as he was variously known, was the natural product of his upbringing. His father, Benjamin Collins (B.C.)

Philip W. Brown Jr., MD
Grandson of A.W. Tillinghast

Tillinghast, attended the U.S. Naval Academy during the Civil War. Unfortunately or not, he had to resign because of illness, presumably tuberculosis, from which he recovered well. (He must have been a very popular fellow for he was invited to the 50th reunion of his class and at the reunion was awarded his class ring.) B.C. was very successful in manufacturing rubber products, the most unusual but best selling of which was a rubber suit for ministers who baptized by immersion. He also was a golfer and wrote poetry for the *American Golfer* under the pen name "Duffer."

B.C. could afford to spoil his son and only child and he certainly did so. A perfect example of this is a photo of young Dadgan, about 8 or 9 years old I guess, in a London zoo riding on the head of Jumbo, the largest elephant ever in captivity. With his face smugly set, his bearing implied that the world owed him obeisance. Although Dagdan's later writing and speech manifested considerable knowledge of the classics, he bragged that he never graduated from any of the several schools that he attended—he either quit

or was thrown out. Perhaps the many overseas trips with his doting parents enriched his knowledge.

In his late teens and early 20's he belonged to a cadre of rogues—wealthy, arrogant, flashy, reckless, heavy drinking playboys. The fashionable Philadelphia Cricket Club, whose golf course he later designed, served as one of their bases of operation.

In 1894, circumstances necessitated his marrying my grandmother, Lillian Quigley (whom we called Damee) a lovely woman quite his junior; to them were born my aunt, Marion, and my mother, Elsie. The financial support of the young family is quite uncertain. It probably came from B.C.'s company, but the company's success was not due to Tillie's time, efforts nor business acumen. He apparently had little interest in it. For instance, the company devised a rubber scraper attached to a wooden, stick—but didn't patent it, much to the delight of Rubbermaid. So after B.C. died in 1918, the company began to wither and as I recall mother closed out the dismal remnant of it in the 1950's.

Dadgan became immersed in golf in 1896 on his first pilgrimage to the celebrated home of golf—St. Andrews. He would return annually for the next five years. Damee accompanied him on all of his golfing jaunts. And it was his great privilege to know Old Tom Morris quite well.

Because of Dagdan's knowledge of golf and the courses of Great Britain, Charles Campbell Worthington, a family friend offered Dagdan the chance to design and supervise the construction of the currently dissembled course at Shawnee-on-the-Delaware in 1909. The course was immediately accorded accolades and served for many tournaments including two on a national scale. With this course and a few others under his belt, he began to make a name in golf course design.

In the early part of the 20th Century, golf was a rich man's sport and it was money that came to seek out Dadgan, not the reverse. And it was big money for the times so Dadgan could thrive on the good things—the chauffeured limousines, the staterooms on trains, the finest of three piece suits, the best tobacco, beautiful antiques to furnish his beautiful house, and the rich and famous with whom he associated. One day when Damee and he were in Mexico City, a somewhat rumpled man hailed him by name. The conversation led to Dadgan inviting him to lunch where the man carried on in heavily accented English. When finally alone, Damee asked who the person was, not having been introduced as was commonly

the case, "Oh some Russian refugee—Leon something— yes, Leon Trotsky."

Dadgan loved his golf even more than he loved the good life. He played it well, very well actually, but erratically. I have a sterling cup that he won in a driving contest. He entered many tournaments including some on a national scale but even if he gained an early lead he rarely would play on to win. He couldn't play consistently enough to go the length. Sometimes he arrived on the first tee quite hung over and on at least one occasion in the remnants of a tuxedo. Once he made a substantial wager that he could use a friend's heirloom pocket watch as a tee and that the watch would never miss a tick. Unfortunately the friend never heard the watch tick again. But worse yet, Dadgan lost a lot of money. Betting and braggadocio were not foreign to our grandfather.

Dagdan quit playing competitive golf abruptly when he lost his amateur standing. His income from writing and golf architecture classified him as a professional by the USGA. In an impetuous, but typical, response to the USGA he wrote: "If such be sin, then I will continue in the ways of sin."

He was so very quick mentally that in short order he usually would dominate any conversation. In this he was aided by an exceptional memory for people and places. He was a superb raconteur and told a lot of jokes, but in mixed company, none that were off color. He also had a fertile imagination and a creative bent for things in which he was interested. For instance, to aid in his work in the field, he invented, he later claimed, the clip board. Naturally he failed to patent it. He enthusiastically played any and all card games and especially loved bridge. He wrote a lot and he wrote well. Some of his short stories Mother considered maudlin, as do I. Yet I see that the USGA has issued a new specially-bound edition of his two books (*The Cobble Valley Yarns* and *The Mutt and Jeff*). His photography was superb. And when it came to designing and supervising construction of a course, he was completely focused and almost indefatigable. An old man once told my sister that when he was young he saw Dadgan advising on a course for the Works Progress Administration. He described Dadgan's imperious mannerisms to a tee, commenting that as he walked around the course he would wave his hickory pointing stick in a grand way and say: "Bunker here!" "Tree there!"

One humorous quip attributed to Dadgan understandably gained currency because it really is clever. When my father asked for mother's hand in marriage, he is alleged to have mentioned his having done well on his tests in medical school. To this Dadgan is purported to have said: "Young man, the only test I'm interested in is your Wassermann Test!"

At any rate, mother and father were married in 1922 and Dadgan loaned them one of his cars for the honeymoon, not any car of course, but a Stutz Bearcat! Enroute, this wondrous luxury machine suffered the ignominy of running into a pig. The consequence to the car – and to the new son-in-law – are unknown. One would suspect that Dadgan simply waived it all off.

Father and Mother established residence in Rochester, Minnesota. And soon thereafter Dagdan designed a gem of a golf course at Rochester Golf & Country Club. This course was built for our family—Father and Mother were members of Rochester and I grew up playing the game there. On behalf of Father and Mother, Dadgan waived his customary fee and asked only for the carfare for Damee and him to visit. The carfare soon became quite a joke, for Dadgan, as usual became quite involved in the course and popped out quite often to see how things were coming

The good times went on. The money rolled in and the money rolled out. The Roaring 20's were roaring and Dadgan was in on the roar. He bought options on 200 acres on the Jersey side of where the George Washington Bridge is now located, but failed to register the deeds. He was a "Broadway Angel" but none of the plays he backed was ever a winner. Prohibition didn't seem to hamper his drinking one bit. And with the times being as they were, there was no reason to save for the future, a future that was unfortunately forecast on a Tuesday in late October 1929, the Black Tuesday when the stock market crashed.

Golf course design was not a Depression-proof occupation. Scheduled payments from courses began to dwindle and the request to design new courses screeched to a halt. Embarrassingly, some personal objects had to be sold and then some more. It was hard to relinquish the good things and the good ways of life. And one certainly must maintain appearances! Eventually, he had to hire out to the W.P.A. to advise on courses. This provided some

income as did some of his writing.

When Mother "took me East" in 1934 at age 5, we stayed in the house in Harrington Park, New Jersey. This house, which would soon "go on the block" along with much of its contents, was set on generous grounds. (It was recently located by the efforts of Louis Chanin of New City, New York.) Lining the wall adjacent to the stairs that gracefully rose to the second floor was a splattering of framed photographs. I learned many years later that these were from the rich and famous, inscribed "To Albert" or "To Bertie with love," from the likes of Lillian Russell, Jack Dempsey, Thomas Alva Edison, and so on. One night, I recall, there was quite a party—a large one with yard lanterns, servants, food and many people. Among them were some Russian nobility who had fled the Bolshevik Revolution some 15 years earlier. Dadgan could never resist a chance to hobnob with the elite, even if they were ex-elite.

Some have claimed that Dadgan's madcaps and escapades have been grossly exaggerated. Having heard my mother's (and my father's) stories over the years, I accept them as probably true for the most part. There is no doubt that he did "take-off" at times. He would simply leave home without any announcement, never for long, perhaps a few days to a week or so, and in no regular fashion. I don't know how often nor over how many years he did this. And what he did and where he went is anybody's guess, but church was not likely on the itinerary. Equally unannounced he would return, offer no explanation for his absence, and resume his usual life. Sometimes, if momentarily short of funds, he would pawn some of Damee's furs and jewelry. When he came upon sufficient funds, he would reclaim most of the items he had hocked, buy something more as a peace offering, and then cycle them all through again.

Dagdan's dark side is best illustrated by one of my mother's recollections. One night, when roused by loud voices, my mother got up and went to the head of the stairs frightened and puzzled by the scene below. Dagdan, apparently drunk was shouting and waving a pistol while Damee held his wrist and shouted back. The what's and why's of this my mother would never know, for apparently she never spoke to either Dagdan or Damee about it. So

our grandfather, who charmed so many people outside the family, created bad relations within it. My mother was afraid of him and found him cold. She disliked being called in to see him in the drawing room and then being dismissed with no warmth or tact. My aunt Marion at one point is said to have detested him. She even gave her little gifts from him to my mother.

At some point he and Damee moved to the Los Angeles area, and in Beverly Hills they started an antique shop in partnership with their friend Nedda Harrigan. Nedda's father was the Harrigan of James M. Cohan's song by that title; Nedda later married director Josh Logan. Dadgan's exquisite taste, his knowledge of asset values, and his proclivity to be a pack rat now stood him in good stead. Over the years he had collected and enjoyed a large number of high quality articles, from furniture (his forte) to glass to artists' sketches or anything else of value that caught his fancy. He may have had to sell them for less than what he paid but at least they kept him going. As there were many people who also had fallen on hard times and were trying to survive, he could buy or broker additional material. He was smart to have gone to Hollywood, as the financiers and other high-rollers were broke but the movie people were still making good money.

Nonetheless the going was tough and then got tougher and finally there was an end to it. Basically everything was gone. At some point in this slide into poverty he changed. Our father had always held Dagdan in limited respect. After all, a toper, a spendthrift, and in general an F. Scott Fitzgerald type did not garner points with a man raised by WCTU (Women's Christian Temperance Union) parents in a remote mining town in Colorado. Additionally, Father's income had also been sharply reduced by the Depression and he had three kids to raise; he was therefore more than a little disgruntled at having to send support money to a once-wealthy father-in-law who was a victim in part of his own extravagance. But Father did say to me on several occasions that he admired Dadgan for the way he responded to this catastrophic reversal of fortunes. Dagdan stopped his drinking, he no longer caroused, he scrambled hard to survive and to my

knowledge never bemoaned his fate.

Dagdan's health may have been a factor in his turn to temperance. Arteriosclerosis in his legs and mild diabetes had been diagnosed in 1936. In 1941 heart disease became sufficiently severe to put him out of commission. He and Damee moved to the home of Aunt Marion in Toledo. There he continued some off and on writing up to his death on May 19, 1942. Being true to family values, Damee remained dedicated to him right to his end, despite his imperious attitude toward her. My cousin recalled that when he would bellow her name from an adjoining room, she would always drop whatever she was doing and hurry to him for whatever need or whim he had at that moment.

My last remembrance of Dadgan is very sketchy. He visited Rochester, Minnesota one hot summer when I must have been 6 or 7, about 1936. I sat in his lap, fearful of the waxed mustache and the scratchiness of the heavy wool 3-piece suit he wore despite the heat of that dust bowl summer. In heavy pencil lines he quickly sketched cartoon figures, which have miraculously survived for 60 years—a Sneezer, a Whiffensnoozer, and others from his fertile imagination. He would make popping noises to which he would ask "Where's Gus?" and most amazingly, he would flip a lighted cigarette inside his mouth, smoke it, and then flip it back out, still lit. Not only can I not design golf courses, but I burned my mouth trying to do that cigarette trick in later years.

Yes, Dadgan had some of Seneca's madness in him, but that made him all the more colorful and attractive to outsiders. Fortunately his creative genius outlived the madness, allowing us to enjoy his courses these many decades later. As golfers then, we are all richer for that genius. And I am grateful to Bob Trebus and Rick Wolffe for this remarkable exposition.

Dr. Philip Brown, Jr. MD
Rochester, MN

Whiffenpoof

Whiffensnoozer.

Sneezer

TILLINGHAST COURSES
ORIGINAL DESIGNS, RECONSTRUCTIONS,

Abington Club
(FKA Old York Road Country Club)
Jenkintown, PA
Alpine Country Club
Alpine, NJ
Anglo-American Club
Lac L'Achign, Quebec
Aronimink Golf Club
Drexel Hill, PA (Extinct)
Atlantic Beach Country Club
Atlantic Beach, FL (Extinct)
Baltimore Country Club, Five Farms East
Baltimore, MD
Baltusrol Lower and Upper
Springfield, NJ
Bass Rocks Golf Club
Gloucester, MA
Beavertail Country Club
Jamestown, RI (Extinct)
Bedford Springs Golf Club
Bedford, PA
Belmont Park Golf Course
(FKA Hermitage Country Club)
Richmond, VA
Berkshire Hills Country Club
Pittsfield, MA
Bethpage State Park Black, Blue, Red, Green and Red
Farmingdale, NY
Binghamton Country Club
Endwell, NY
Blackhawk Country Club
Madison, WI
Bluff Point Golf & Country Club
Plattsburg, NY
Bonnie Briar Country Club
Larchmont, NY
Brackenridge Park Golf Course
San Antonio, TX
Brook Hollow Golf Club
Dallas, TX
Brooklawn Country Club
Fairfield, CT
Brookside Golf Course
Pasadena, CA

Cherokee Golf Course
Louisville, KY
Country Club of Fairfield
Fairfield, CT
Country Club of Ithaca
Ithaca, NY (Extinct)
Cedar Crest Golf Course
Dallas, TX
Cedarbrook Country Club
Philadelphia, PA (Extinct)
Corsicana Country Club
Corsicana, TX
Crescent Hill Golf Course
Louisville, KY
Dallas Country Club
Dallas, TX
Davis Shores Country Club
St. Augustine, FL
Elm Ridge Country Club
Montreal, Quebec (Extinct)
Elmira Country Club
Elmira, NY
Elmwood Country Club
White Plains, NY
Essex County Country Club
West Orange, NJ
Fenway Golf Club
Scarsdale, NY
Forest Hill Field Club
Bloomfield, NJ
Fort Sam Houston Golf Club
La Oma Course
Fort Sam Houston, TX
Fort Worth Country Club
Fort Worth, TX
Fox Hill Country Club
Exeter, PA
Framingham Country Club
Framingham, MA
Francis Byrne Golf Course
West Orange, NJ
Fresh Meadow Country Club
Flushing, NY (Extinct)
Galen Hall Country Club
Wernersville, PA
Glen Oak Country Club
Glen Ellyn, IL

Glen Ridge Country Club
Glen Ridge, NJ
Golden Valley Country Club
Golden Valley, MN
Hackensack Golf Club
Oradell, NJ
Harmon Country Club
Lebanon, NY
Hempstead Golf Club
Hempstead, NY
Illinois Golf Club
Glen Cove, IL (Extinct)
Indian Hills Country Club
Mission Hills, KS
Inverness Club
Toledo, OH
Irem Temple Country Club
Dallas, PA
Island Hills Golf Club
Sayville, NY
Jackson Heights Country Club
Jamaica, NY (Extinct)
Johnson City Country Club
Johnson City, TN
Kansas City Country Club
Shawnee Mission, KS
Kingsport Country Club
Kingsport, TN (Extinct)
Knollwood Country Club
Elmsford, NY
Lakewood Country Club
Westlake, OH
Marble Island Golf Club
Colchester, VT
Meadowbrook Country Club
Northville, MI
Meadow Brook Hunt Club
Westbury, NY (Extinct)
Metropolis Country Club
White Plains, NY
Mount Kisco Country Club
Mount Kisco, NY
Myers Park Country Club
Charlotte, NC
Myosotis Country Club
Eatontown, NJ (Extinct)

EXPANSIONS AND ADDITIONS

Nemacolin Country Club
Beallsville, PA
New Castle Country Club
New Castle, PA
Newport Country Club
Newport, RI
Niagara Falls Country Club
Lewiston, NY
North Hempstead Country Club
Port Washington, NY
North Shore Country Club
Glen Head, NY
Norwood Country Club
Long Branch, NJ (Extinct)
Oak Hills Country Club
(FKA Alamo Country Club)
San Antonio, TX
Oaks Country Club
Tulsa, OK
Old Oaks Country Club
Purchase, NY
Oswego Country Club
Oswego, NY
Philadelphia Cricket Club
Philadelphia, PA
Pine Valley Golf Club
Clementon, NJ
Pittsburgh Field Club
Pittsburgh, PA
Pontousuk Lake Country Club
Pittsfield, MA
Port Jervis Country Club
Port Jervis, NY
Poxono Country Club
Shawnee-On-Delaware, PA
Quaker Ridge Golf Club
Scarsdale, NY
Rainey Estate Golf Club
Huntington, NY
Ridgewood Country Club
Paramus, NJ
Roanoke Country Club
Roanoke, VA
Rochester Golf & Country Club
Rochester, MN
Rockaway Hunting Club
Cedarhurst, NY

Rock Hill Country Club
Rock Hill, SC
Rockwood Hall Country Club
Tarrytown, NY (Extinct)
San Antonio Country Club
San Antonio, TX
San Francisco Golf Club
San Francisco, CA
Sands Point Golf Club, Middle
Sands Point, NY
Sankaty Head Golf Club
Siasconset, MA
Sauganash Country Club
Three Rivers, MI
Scarboro Golf & Country Club
Toronto, Canada
Scarsdale Golf Club
Hartsdale, NY
Seaview Golf Club, Bay Course
Absecon, NJ
Seneca Golf Course
Louisville, KY
Shackamaxon Country Club
Westfield, NJ
Shawnee Country Club
Shawnee-On-Delaware, PA
Shawnee Golf Course
Louisville, KY
Shreveport Country Club
Shreveport, LA
Sleepy Hollow Country Club
Scarborough, NY
Somerset Hills Country Club
Bernardsville, NJ
Southward Ho Country Club
Bayshore, NY
Spring Lake Golf Club
Spring Lake, NJ
St. Albans Country Club
St. Albans, NY
St. Davids Golf Club
Wayne, PA
St. Petersburg Country Club
St. Petersburg (Davista), FL
Suburban Country Club
Pikesville, MD

Suburban Golf Club
Union, NJ
Sunnehanna Country Club
Johnston, PA
Sunningdale Country Club
Scarsdale, NY
Suneagles Golf Club, at Fort Monmouth
Eatontown, NJ
Swope Memorial Golf Course
Kansas City, MO
The Country Club
Minneapolis, MN
Tulsa Country Club
Tulsa, OK
Upper Montclair Country Club
Clifton, NJ (Extinct)
Valley Country Club
Conyngham, PA
Virginia Country Club
Long Beach, CA
Wanango Country Club
Reno, PA
Westmoreland Country Club
Wilmette, IL
Westwood Country Club
Clayton, MO
Williamsport Country Club
Williamsport, PA
Winged Foot West and East
Mamaroneck, NY
Wolferts Roost Country Club
Albany, NY
Wykagyl Country Club
New Rochelle, NY
Wyoming Valley Country Club
Wilkes Barre, PA

For more information on course specific designs and revisions see:
1) *The Architects of Golf*, Geoffrey S. Cornish and Ronald E. Whitten, 1993
2) "Golf's Forgotten Genius," *Golf Journal*, Frank Hannigan, 1974

1

THE IDEAL COURSE RUGGED AND NATURAL

FOR a good many years back it has been my extremely pleasant business to select locations for golf courses, prepare the plans and frequently to supervise their actual construction. Naturally my eye is peeled, as the saying goes, for impressively outstanding natural features. These are many but, of them all, I am sure that none moves me to greater enthusiasm than do sand dunes, big dunes contoured through the years by sweeping winds, and set off by wild grasses and drifted sands. And while we do succeed in approaching nature by artificial means so frequently we are in utter despair in the realization of the utter futility of imitating the primitive contours and sweeps of the dunes. True enough we have come rather close to *it*, but in my eyes there seems always to be lacking an indefinable something as the artificial work proclaims that it was made by man.

Consequently when we find the areas of sand dunes on or about the sites of proposed courses, it is peculiarly gratifying. And this is only too seldom in roaming over a continent as broad as ours for the dunes bespeak the sea and the approaches to it as a general rule. There they belong and it would be bad taste to attempt to reproduce them artificially along a sylvan fairway, far inland and away from their native heaths. However a thought of the rugged contours will relieve formality of lines when hazards are constructed anywhere.

No doubt my own appreciation of these rough fellows

Here is nature's model and no artifice of man can equal the beauty of it.

dates back into the latter part of the last century, some years before I took up golf course architecture, when it was an annual habit of mine to visit and play over some of the sea-side courses in Great Britain. There the dunes were so much a part of the golf picture that I could not bring myself to visualize a course without looking at it through the irregular contours of sandy hillocks and the whins. These were traditional with the game itself, its origin and its growth.

Long Island, particularly out near its end, appeals to me as one of the most fortunate sections imaginable for golf course creation, or probably it would be much better to say—course development from natural creation. There you will find dunes in plenty. As Findlay Douglas once remarked to me—"There are thousands of natural golf courses out towards Montauk Point." And I know he was right.

But no doubt many of the hazard-shirking fraternity would declare that playing a wayward ball from such places was entirely too difficult. What utter nonsense! There were and are shots that will do it; another generation knew how to play them, and it is not altogether pleasant to think that golfers of today are going soft. Possibly a bit more of sting in the rod of golf chastisement in these, our modern times, would render it more of an achievement to break par so habitually.

The Shawnee Country Club at Shawnee-on-Delaware.

San Antonio's Civic Course. Here and there, above the Mesquite and the Huisache, towered these gigantic Pecan trees.

Beginning work on a pot bunker at Shawnee Country Club.

The Punch Bowl green (12th hole) at Shawnee Country Club.

18

2

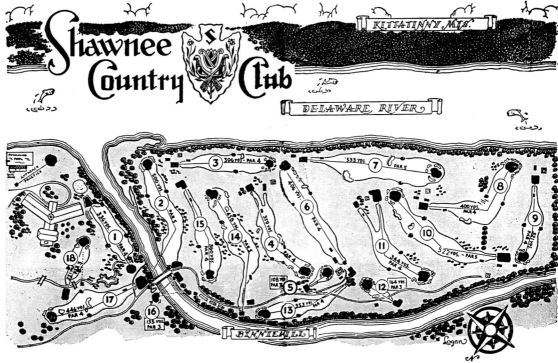

ALTHOUGH the recognized round of golf calls for the play of eighteen holes, custom has rather divided it in half and generally the score cards separate the two nines, designating them as the Out and In journeys. First thought would prompt the explanation that the full round was divided in this manner because of the former predominance of nine-hole courses, over which two rounds (each alike) had to be played before the complete round was finished. But many of the famous old courses provided eighteen holes, frequently with the ninth at an extreme corner, remote from the clubhouse, and from this point the play, which had been Out, or away, turned and came In, or home. For this reason the Turn was reached after the ninth green had been quit.

That the Turn exerts a pronounced psychological influence cannot be questioned. Some literally play their heads off until the Turn is reached and then they seem to crumple up and perform on the home journey in a distinctly inferior manner. Some quit running when the Turn is reached, while others find their feet and speed briskly away from the ruts and rough going of the first nine holes. Probably you have noticed that your own play often is influenced by the thought of the Turn. Maybe you have sneaked in a bad hole or two at the start and, as the disgusting figures are recorded, you realize that the hoped for score "going Out" has been ruined, and you mentally register the vow that you will make up for it "going In." Instead of pulling yourself together on the spot you continue playing the next few holes to the Turn in a shockingly listless mood, but on the tenth teeing ground a new light comes to the eye and you plainly show by every word and move that you are going to make every one sit up and take notice on the way Home.

"I was out in 39, but it took me 50 to come home!"
"Then, why didn't you stay out?"

This wheeze and others like the well-known Grand Army pun, each honorably ancient, were born at the Turn. In the old days, beyond recall, the half-way house was always located there, not because it happened to be the geographical center of the course, but because it was without a doubt the best place to dispense stimulants, for at the ninth-and-a-half hole elation and depression rose and ebbed to an extent only slightly less than at the nineteenth. So if I have sufficiently established the traditional importance of the Turn, may I regard it from the field of the course architect?

19

3 WHAT IS GOLF COURSE ARCHITECTURE?

SOMETIMES we hear this question: "What is golf architecture?" It may be answered in few words. In the old days, when a club desired a course, there would be called in a professional player who would have very little time to give to the work, and he would be expected to know instinctively where the hole should be placed. He might walk over the ground once or twice, and after the third walk, the course would be laid out. He has done the best that he could in the short time which he has, but, after all, he only has been able to locate the greens and give a general idea of the run of the course.

The modern golf architect devotes many days to exhaustive study of conditions; the ground must be surveyed and charted, and greens and hazards are modeled in miniature before work is begun. The conscientious builder of courses desires to spend a great deal of his time on the ground as the work progresses, for often there are slight eleventh hour changes to be made. It is unfair to criticize the work of some professionals, for they are players, and even though they have given the laying out of courses some study, they cannot devote the time which is necessary to the construction of a modern course.

Besides having a profound knowledge of the strokes of golf and the groups of strokes which should be demanded by a modern course, the architect must be something of an engineer. Greens cannot be placed always in spots which look attractive, for possibly these spots would not produce good turf.

The character of soil and drainage must be given much attention. However, I think that it is not possible to lay out a golf course by theory alone. The architect must be a player with a feel of the shots. To be sure, there are times when the first judgments may be wrong. He conceives a drive and mid-iron hole, but after it has been surveyed and he gets the actual distance, he finds that it is longer than he anticipated—possibly a drive and cleek, or drive and brassey length; but usually the first judgment of the expert is nearly correct. It is the feel of the shots rather than the measure of tape that is the greatest asset to the builder of courses.

Wherever the construction of a golf course is contemplated, it is desirable that an expert advise in the

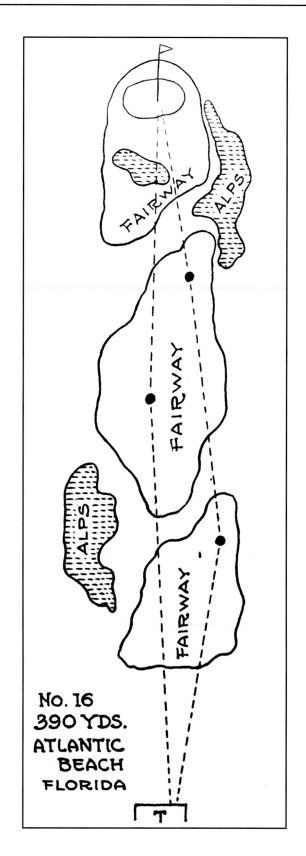

NO. 16
390 YDS.
ATLANTIC
BEACH
FLORIDA

selection of ground for a proposed course. In his eyes the undeveloped ground is a finished creation, and his experience enables him to determine immediately the most promising site. A modern course requires from one hundred to one hundred and fifty acres, although in some instances, when the tracts have been spread out considerably, very satisfactory lay-outs have placed eighteen holes on a trifle less than ninety acres. Then, step by step:

Permit a golf architect of recognized repute to plan the course. There are many possible arrangements on every tract, but he will determine the best one.

Call in a green-keeper and constructor of unquestioned merit. Place in his hands the prints and models prepared by your architect.

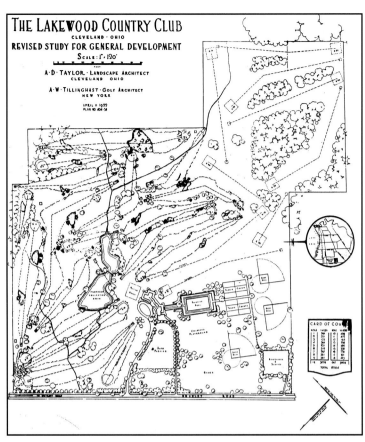

Permit your constructor to follow the plans unhampered and without the slightest interference.

Adhere unwaveringly to the expert advice which you have paid for, and use only materials of known and tested excellence.

It is my purpose to illustrate types of modern holes, and in this article there is shown one from the course at Atlantic Beach, Florida. The segregated fairways are distinctly modern, and they are particularly effective in sandy country. The islands of green, standing out prominently in the midst of the surrounding sand, not only are pleasing to the eye, but provide very sound golf.

Of course the expert will play directly on to the middle fairway, which enables him to be home with his second, a feat beyond the powers of the short driver, who places his tee shot on the first fairway.

The tenth green at Atlantic Beach, FL. The entire eighteen holes was opened for play in 1915.

4 WHAT GOLFERS ARE DEMANDING OF THE ARCHITECT

WHEN the golf club of the present day decides to build a new course or to reconstruct an old one, naturally enough there is considerable interest displayed by the players who anticipate playing many rounds over the new lay-out. A golf architect is consulted and when he arrives on the scene he is pretty sure to be told of individual ideas and preferences. Usually a number of the golfers recall certain excellent holes which have inspired their play over other courses in various sections. Frequently these suggestions are resented by a few of the profession, but personally I like to her them, for it indicates that the players of today are thoughtful and analytical and rather sure to appreciate good work.

The Dean of American Born Architects

Fifteen years ago the architect was not altogether welcomed by an element which inclined to believe that the old course was quite good enough as it was. They grumbled when the green committee consulted an architect and freely expressed the fear that the so-called improving of their playing conditions really meant the making of them so much harder and exacting that the golf would cease to be a pleasure for all excepting a few low handicap men. This element of doubting Thomases is not so often encountered as of yore. Now general character of modern holes is widely known and understood and players everywhere appreciate that intelligent treatment of holes does not make play any more exasperating to those of average skill or even mediocre ability.

But the rank and file do make demands of the architect and it is only proper that they should, for they are paying for the work and they surely have a perfect right to be assured that their money is not being wasted nor applied to constructing freak holes. They demand that their play shall be something other than pulling one trick after another out of the bag. They demand good, honest golf but are not at all adverse to spectacular holes which are sound; as a matter of fact golfers generally like bold holes, which stand out impressively. And in nearly every instance, when a new course is being planned there is great demand for a good water hole or even more than one.

In the inspection of a plan, either on a chart or on the ground, the players want to be convinced that there are no deadly parallels of fairway or no points where there is unnecessary danger. Very long walks from putting-green to teeing-ground are not liked. The obvious advantage of having the first and the tenth teeing-grounds, and the ninth and the eighteenth putting-greens in close proximity to the clubhouse is recognized in all sections of the country and the architect is requested to plan this end if at all possible.

The preservation of fine trees is a very usual demand and golfers are showing an appreciation of beautiful scenic effects to a far greater degree than ever before. The days of sitting aside complacently while the architect goes ahead serenely alone are of the past. Clubmen of golf today want to know what is doing. They like to visit the grounds often to criticize and suggest. I recall the building of an important course some years since and the occasions when any of the large membership took the trouble to look over the work were few indeed. They seemed satisfied to wait patiently until the new course was thrown open for play. In contrast, a new course is building now and a few weeks ago over forty members went over the entire course with the architect on one afternoon and they were not at all backward about asking questions. This is as it should be.

Men who golf should have ideas of their own. Often the suggestions are of little or no use to the architect, but frequently they are sound and of real value. Don't be afraid to ask your architect questions, for if he is a true master of his craft he will not only welcome them but also discuss them. Surely I have had some queer theories advanced and some truly absurd suggestions have prompted a short answer. It is a bad habit and as I grow older I am trying to break it.

Some of the best comments of golf holes have been offered by men who are not particularly good players. Indeed, there are expert golfers who are absolutely lacking in imagination and in any faculty of analysis. They can play a hole and tell whether it is good or bad but that is all. But I recall one man, whom I believe had never hit a golf ball in his life, although he had been a close observer of play over many courses for years. His ideas were excellent in many respects. He never could have planned a satisfactory course in its entirety, for assuredly this can only be done by a player of long experience and one who possesses the feel of the shots as well as the vision of them, yet his observation as work progressed were extremely helpful. The actual number of golfers in America is more or less a matter of estimate, but this fact may not be even open to debate—the great majority have but little skill as compared with the comparatively few stellar performers, but this ever increasing army, which plays for the love of the game without any thought of championships, are the men who are making the building of courses everywhere possible and certainly they should not stand in the background with tongues between their teeth when it comes to telling the golf architect what kind of courses provide their greatest joys.

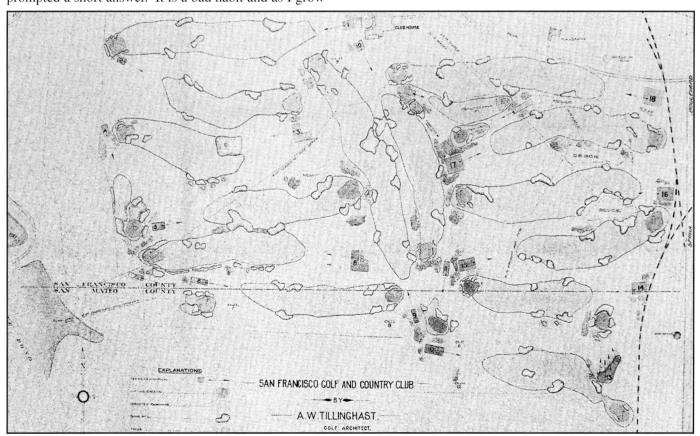

5 Planning the Golf course

BEFORE the golf course architect can lay out a single hole he must know to a certainty the exact site of the clubhouse. This is his dominant, the Alpha and Omega in any event, since wherever possible the course starts and finishes close by the club house, but swings back with the ninth hole and away again with the tenth. The advantages of this arrangement are obvious. Often enough a player desires to cover only nine holes, and if the finish of these were not in the vicinity of the club house he would be forced to end his abbreviated round at a remote corner, or to "cut in" to avoid a monotonous trudge. The two swings of nine holes makes it possible to get the players away over both, on days when the attendance is unusually heavy, and thus relieve congestion in a measure; and it must be remembered that there are many who like to lounge around the grounds and watch the play; bring more play under their observation, and the bettor the spectators are pleased.

Probably it has not occurred to some that it is desirable to turn in the direction of home with the second hole. True, the advantage of this might only be apparent on tournament occasions, when matches go to extra holes, and even if three had to be played, the contestants would find themselves not very far from the clubhouse at the conclusion.

The arrangements which the preceding paragraphs outline are greatly to be desired, but certainly it is the height of folly to force the plan of the holes to attain them, if the scheme detracts from the merits of course. Many of the most famous links in the world keep running away from the clubhouse, which is seen no more until the last putt has been holed. There is another arrangement, a 27-hole scheme, which makes it very necessary to place the club house at the dead center of three swings of nine holes each. This permits various combinations of holes, which add much to the variety of play. For example, during one week swings A and B would combine the main course, leaving C open for overflow; the following week A and C combine, leaving B open; and the next combination of B and C leaves A for the shorter round. It is plainly evident that this arrangement permits of only one selection for the club house site.

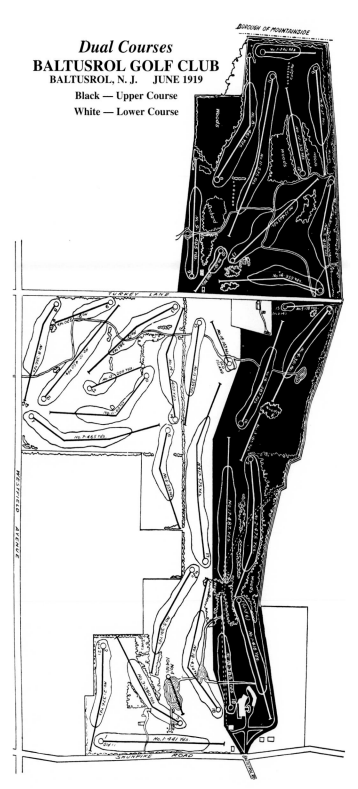

Dual Courses
BALTUSROL GOLF CLUB
BALTUSROL, N. J.   JUNE 1919
Black — Upper Course
White — Lower Course

In recent years some of the large organizations have found it necessary to construct 36 holes. A number of such course were given to me for planning and development. Each necessitated a different arrangement. For example at Baltusrol there stood the magnificent club house at the fag end of the property, and consequently both the Upper and Lower courses have the "turn" at distant points. But close by both ninth greens there stands a building which serves as a halfway house, with telephones

Tudor type harmonizes beautifully and restfully with the surroundings. But it is not concerning the plans of the club house that I have been asked to write briefly; it is of the selection of sites strictly from the viewpoint of the golf architect.

Generally I believe that the presence of an old House or a mansion proves a distinct handicap. Often this sways the committee in the purchase of property. After all, it may be located unfortunately, so far as the demands of golf are

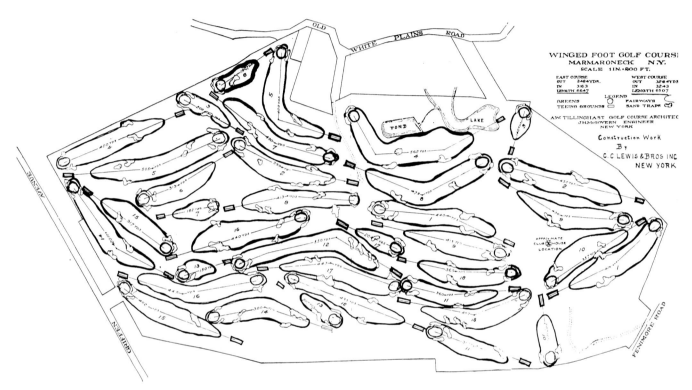

and similar conveniences. The two new courses of the Baltimore Country Club find one course with two swings and the other running straight away from start to finish. Here again there was no choice of a site for the club house, for a fine mansion almost on the south boundary of the property could not be ignored.

However, when the two courses of the "Winged Foot." at Mamaroneck, were planned, the holes were laid out only after the selection of the club house site had been given careful study. Here both the East and West courses offer two swings each, to and from the house, and there also is ample room for a large driving practice area and an unusually generous practice putting course. The views over the Winged Foot courses from the club house are inspiring, and there is every opportunity for spectators on the lawns and verandas to look over play in every direction. Here is a model, and the new building in the

concerned, and with few exceptions these residences, after they are remodeled, are not nearly so adequate as entirely new buildings, planned and located to provide comfort for the golfer of today.

In nine instances out of ten the committee already has a preconceived idea of the proper building site, and in as many cases that site is on a little hilltop at the very greatest elevation on the tract. It is not the intent to question the wisdom of this choice except as it relates to the golf course itself. When club houses are built on unusual elevations it makes it difficult to construct true holes to and from them. Either there is a tendency to get away with a hole, which rather suggests driving off the roof, or the last hole presents blindness; and only too frequently there is also involved that great abomination—an arduous trudge uphill, which brings the players home blowing like porpoises in a state of exhaustion. Personally, I incline to sites at lower levels. I recall discussing this point with two of the leading landscape architects in America—A.D. Taylor of Cleveland and Charles W. Leavitt of New York, who both agreed with me. Mr. Leavitt was developing a tract of some 400 acres for the Philadelphia Cricket Club. It was my work to plan 36 holes there, but before any plans could be attempted it was vital that the club house site be fixed. The committee strongly considered a hilltop, but Mr. Leavitt urged a much lower level. It was his idea to build the entrance roads along the higher levels, so that really the first view of the club house might be had by looking down into a small, sheltered valley, very much after the old English manner. He finally demonstrated that there was more

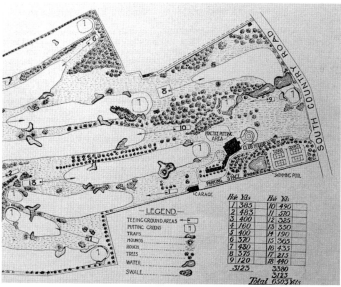

Portion of Golf Course Plan showing two swings of nine holes from Club House site: Southward Ho Country Club, Long Island.

breeze down there than on the hilltop. To be sure, the scenic beauty of any site must be considered to some extent, but golf values are of even greater importance.

The presence of fine trees, brooks and lakes, or the advantages of a particularly inspiring panoramic view, are to be greatly desired, but if they do not happen to be found around the site which lends itself best to the golf course, turn steadfastly away, even though it be what seems at first a less attractive area; for a little imagination may enable one to visualize a future development, when many features have been added with the assistance of a master of landscaping. When the course of Somerset Hills Country Club was built at Bernardsville, N.J., where there were many exceedingly

The Baltimore Country Club's Five Farms Clubhouse.

inviting sites for the club house, the house was finally built where it served the best interests of the course, and it is regarded today as one of the most charming in America. The architect of the house made a great feature of a fine old apple tree at the center of courtyard. It is probable that few people had ever noticed that apple tree before.

When a site is selected, of course due consideration must be paid to the locating of driveways, motor parking spaces, putting lawns, and all that goes to make the country club attractive to players and spectators alike. The holes of the golf course must not encroach too closely on the house and grounds, for when men, and women too, go to the country for relaxation they want to have breathing space, so to speak. The architect of the golf course should confer with the architect of the house and with the architect of the landscaping. "Every shoemaker to his own last," as this is a day of specialists. By working together in harmony, each at his own craft, the hit-or-miss methods of country club building should be relegated to the past even more effectively than they are at present. Many indeed are the golf and country clubs, where, owing to such cooperation, grounds and buildings have been planned and constructed in ways which satisfy the eye as to architectural harmony and afford every detail of physical comfort, thus adding to the pleasure of golfing.

6 THE HOME HOLE

UNDOUBTEDLY the last, the Home hole, should be one of the most exacting of any. No matter what its character may be, the hole must demand precise judgment and accurate execution. Under no circumstance may it be of the length that allows one man to half hit a shot and get home with an opponent, who has hit his. I like to see the Home hole looming up from the teeing ground in a mighty, impressive way. When a match arrives there on even terms, let that hole reward the courageous. There is more yellow spilled all over the teeing grounds of good Home holes than at any other spot on the course.

The Great Rolling Home Green of the West Course at Winged Foot Golf Club. This green must be boldly approached or the first terrace leaves the ball short.

7

GIVING INDIVIDUALITY TO GOLF HOLES

ANY THEATRICAL PRODUCER will tell you that the successful performer must possess talent primarily, and to an almost equal degree personality. Without an appealing personality, a magnetism which draws the audience across the footlights, the actor must be endowed with rare ability to "get his stuff over"—as they say. But with talent, plus personality, the reward of spontaneous, sincere applause is assured. A salesman of any commodity may offer for trade, wares of undoubted excellence, but if he lacks the faculty of making the buyer like him personally he will find it hard sledding to market his merchandise. A wholesome, inspiring individuality goes a long way to make the man. The golf hole should have it just the same as a human.

For no good reason the green committees throughout the country ceased nominating the holes other than by numbers, and to many it seemed that the units of our courses had fallen from the caste of gentility to that of the criminal. Good, honest John Mann might just as suddenly have become convict 41144, and with as little cause, as did (let us say, for example) the famous Arena when the score cards, possibly with ink saving excuse, gave it a number, and robbed of its good name the fine old hole became plain Sixteen, and dragged through the years in lock-step with the others. There were good reasons for calling the hole Arena, and there was none other like it. Everywhere golfers knew of its renown, and many could tell you of the beauties of the hole itself, yet might hesitate in the

Illustrating the character which is given by the treatment of such a feature. Bearing the cognomen of the "Elm," this hole on Winged Foot's West Course has gained a significance through its name which it otherwise might not enjoy.

naming of the course which contained it. As Sixteen it lost much of its identity, and became one of the many sixteens.

In the last few years the naming of holes is becoming general, and certainly the return of the old custom is welcome. However, there should be some real and appropriate reason for the bestowing of a name. It may be recalled, with almost as little reason in the old days Westward Ho! was tagged at the first opportunity to a hole shooting into the west, although it was bad enough to play a sun-hole without calling attention to the fact that it pointed in a mighty mean direction. There should be names for golf holes, but let them be significant and unique. The plains Indians never named their children until some incident in the child's life suggested a fitting one. Frequently the real name waited until the individual was advanced in youth, or even a warrior, as was the case with Plenty Coups and Young Man Afraid of His Horses. Not that we might pattern the names of golf holes after the red men in fact, but there must be some outstanding feature or incident that will give to a hole an individuality that none other may enjoy. This brings me to the real point of my article by possibly a devious path.

Let every hole be worthy of a name. If it does not possess a striking individuality through some gift of Nature, it must be given as much as possible artificially, and the artifice must be introduced in so subtle a manner as to make it seem natural. The photograph of the Elm hole shows one to which a name fastened itself immediately. Often a hole will name itself as this one did. The fine elm beyond the green lends a charming individuality to the hole, which would have been totally missing had this tree been felled. Yet the surroundings of the green in the virgin state presented nothing of the present effect. As a matter of fact, there were many trees at this place—most of them worthless, to be sure, but quite sufficient to hide most of the beauty of the splendid specimen that stands alone, its solitary vigil suggesting a sentinel, which by the way might have been an equally appropriate name. Probably it is a good example of lending dignity to a hole with the aid of Nature. In my humble opinion the smaller companion elm, which was removed, would have destroyed the beauty in this particular instance.

Often a name will attach itself, and did so even in the days when numbers were used almost exclusively. This was a fact at Shawnee, which course I had the honor of planning. There the present sixteenth has never been known by any appellation other than the Binniekill. This hole is individual to a marked degree, and it is almost entirely natural. The shot is ordinarily a mashie and entirely across water, which feature made a remarkably impressive hole of one which otherwise would have been commonplace. Certainly there are better holes at Shawnee than the Binniekill, but not one remains longer in the memory of the golfing pilgrim than this wee one which happens at such a fortunate time in the round; for there is no better place for a good short hole than at the sixteenth when the close match is drawing to its end and nerves are taut with accuracy at a tremendous premium.

This reference to the unusual appeal and individuality of a good water hazard warrants the inclusion of a particularly fine Photograph of one of the new holes of the Winged Foot Golf Club of the New York Athletic Club at Mamaroneck, in Westchester County, New York. This has

The "Old Soak" bears a very obvious name. Many a mistimed shot will find a liquid grave there.

been christened Old Soak, for reasons which are obvious. It is worthy of a brief description, since the natural features are unusual and impressive. In the first place, two separate lakes are used in the plan. The drive crosses the first lake, offering a graded elective carry. The extremely long player may reach far enough to take a full "soak" with his brassey across the second lake to the green. (The photograph was taken from a point near the green looking back along this shot which would cross the water at a point over the two felled trees.) But ordinarily the hole will be a three-shotter, with the second along the second lake to open up the green to an accurate approach. It will be interesting to know that as a two-shotter the hole will call for about four hundred and sixty yards, which none other than the most courageous smiters will attempt, while the three-shot player will cover nearly a hundred yards more. The possibility of finding either of the two lakes is a further warrant for its name.

Certain it is that the water holes are popular. There is the mental hazard as the great factor, and the average golfer likes to court danger occasionally, provided the architect gives him a safer way around if desired, but probably they meet with so much favor because they generally are attractive to look upon, with a marked individuality. To be sure, there are so-called water holes which are little more than frog ponds, covered with slime and stagnant, where the *larvae* of the mosquito thrive. These represent faulty construction, and usually reveal outlets badly clogged with vegetation. It is not difficult to introduce the water hazard, and another article deals with them in detail. They are discussed now wholly as outstanding features which go so far to make the course beautiful. They offer a distinct change from the holes over meadowlands, which so frequently are monotonous and featureless, and entirely without reason—for there is absolutely no excuse for a featureless hole anywhere on any course. A round of golf should present eighteen inspirations—not necessarily thrills, for spectacular holes may be sadly overdone. Every hole may be constructed to provide charm without being obtrusive with it. When I speak of a hole being inspiring, it is not intended to infer that the visitor is to be subject to attacks of hysteria on every teeing ground as he casts his eye over the fairway to the green for the first time, and to be so overwhelmed with the outstanding features, both natural and manufactured, that he can not keep his eye on the ball. It must be remembered that the great majority of golfers are aiming to reduce their previous best performance by five strokes if possible, first, last and all the time, and if any one of them arrives at the home teeing-ground with this possibility in reach, he is not caring two hoots whether he is driving off from nearby an ancient oak of majestic size and form or a dead sassafras. If his round ends happily it is one beautiful course. Such is human nature.

But in every human there lurks somewhere the admiration of the beautiful, and there are few, indeed, who are so callused that the emphasized features of a golf hole will not sink in somewhere and make him enjoy his round, even though it is subconscious. Let us suppose, for example, that there happens to be a fine old apple tree near a teeing ground, where sometimes players may have to wait. It is more than likely that the architect has so arranged the hole that the old tree is featured there, and a circular bench has been built around the tree. Maybe someone, who has closed his desk in town and taken to the links for real recreation, sits there and as he waits the old tree suddenly seems friendly—and maybe he recalls just such a tree from which, years ago, a small boy filled his shirt with apples, all the while ready to cut and run if the farmer happened along. With that memory, no matter if the round runs into three figures, the afternoon's golf has been something more than a game after all.

The crack players demand real testing holes. This is entirely as it should be, but they, too, will find a new sting to their shots if the surroundings make them feel that they are playing no common, low-down hole. No hole need be formal and ugly to be a true test of playing ability. The National Links offers one of the hardest tests of the game in the world, and the course is beautiful and inspiring. It represents the exact opposite of the inland course, and its treatment is a monument to its creator.

During the past fifteen years the writer has come in contact with thousands who have their own ideas concerning courses. During the last five years these lay ideas were advanced in great numbers and along different lines than formerly. In every section of the country the demand is for sound courses, but above all they want the beautiful. To be frank, half the time the builders of new courses have no ideas concerning the character of the holes or their distribution, and without hesitation put this squarely up to the architect, trusting to his reputation to produce something which will be worthy. But the men who play generally do have very pronounced thoughts concerning the general character of the course as a whole. They ask for holes which will give them pleasure to play, and nine times in ten there is the dominating thought of the beauties of the course. The study of these desires seems to be the real secret of modern course building, and one cannot conceive any hole which is not featured along well-defined lines which every hole must suggest naturally. In planning eighteen holes there are thousands of combinations, each offering a mute appeal for recognition. It is necessary, of course, to decide on the collection which will work out economically and satisfactorily from many angles. But this is sure: every hole must have individuality and be sound. Often it is necessary to get from one section to another over ground which is not suited to the easiest construction, but that troublesome hole must be made to stand right up in meeting with the others, and if it has not got anything about it that might make it respectable, it has got to have quality knocked into it until it can hold its head up in polite society.

Many committees are returning to the old custom of naming the holes of their courses. To me this was always pleasing and when the practice disappeared generally, I was very loath to see it pass. Now there is a revival. Many courses are changed from time to time. Sometimes the committee deems it wise to change the playing order. When this is done, immediately the holes are difficult to remember when discussing them, apart from the links.

The most famous holes on British courses were referred to by names: The Redan at North Berwick, for example; the Station Master's Garden at St. Andrews. Everywhere they were known by these names, and they still are. It is not because the custom is followed in Great Britain that I advocate it, but because it is sensible. The naming of a good hole certainly adds to its distinction. It gives it an individuality. One of the first of American Clubs to return to the old custom was the Somerset Hills Country Club. Mr. C. Ledyard Blair was responsible for it and it is to be hoped that his example is followed by others. Already I have heard of a number of instances where it is to be done.

The thirteenth at George Crump's demanding Pine Valley: I was one of the first to walk the property with him, and that George Crump finally incorporated two of my conceptions entirely, the long seventh and the thirteenth, will ever be the source of great satisfaction.

The famous Binnikill hole at Shawnee: Walter Hagen is standing at the edge of the green.

8 THE CLUBHOUSE

Baltusrol's magnificent clubhouse harmonizes with its courses.

DO MEN TURN to their country clubs from the whirl of the city to find the atmosphere of the city in their club houses? Certainly they go to golf but after an afternoon in the fields with the country-side or sea stretching before them, they are likely to lose a bit of charm if they walk immediately into a corridor which strikingly resembles another in a typically modern city hotel.

In my humble opinion the club room should reflect the character of the immediate outdoors, almost to the extent that the course itself should be a part of its surroundings. The very air should be redolent with the atmosphere of the community. In the club house by the sea what could be more restful than suggestions of ocean and wind-swept shores. Surely a picture of a lone sand dune, hanging on the wall, would be more to the point here than one showing a sunrise over the Matterhorn. In the mountains let us be reminded of hoot-owls and pines rather than gulls

and drift-wood. Surely the fact that the club room of the inland course must find a distinct charm if it makes very real a memory of other farm houses of which the recollection of the mingled odors of apple-butter, calicoes, burning apple wood, hound dogs and lavender has been only a vagrant, elusive sensation as the years have passed.

I am a very strong advocate for appropriate club houses-after suitable golf courses. There can be no question as to which is the more important. There are a number of hundred-thousand-dollar club houses on the edge of thirty-cent-courses. By all means consider the proper development of the course first. Some of the greatest courses have very modest club houses indeed. They are comfortable enough to be sure, with large, well lighted and ventilated locker rooms, but the buildings are not at all pretentious. Of course the selection of the site is of vital importance, but many courses have been ruined from the start by forcing the holes to fit around a spot which is of unfortunate selection. Too often the course has to play second fiddle.

There comes to mind the situation of a certain club, which arrived at the very proper realization that its course was antiquated and poor. A golf architect was retained to make recommendations. Owing to conditions, which absolutely prevented extensions in the direction of north and south, he was forced to the conclusion that no changes, however elaborate they might be, could bolster the course to anything like an ideal plan. The ground contours were atrocious, and the old course represented a most unfortunate selection. His report analyzed conditions thoroughly, and despite the fact that there was a fairly imposing clubhouse to be considered, he advised the club to waste no money in any improvement of the course, because the results could not possibly justify the great expense. The committee was advised to seek new property in the vicinity, where a course of distinction could be created. But the clubhouse caused them to balk. As a matter of fact, the building is not ideal and it could be remodeled for a residence, yet there it is today, apparently, an unsurmountable obstacle to the permanent life of the club as a real factor in golf.

When the "Apple Tree Gang," the fathers of American golf, started to play, they hung their coats on the branches of a convenient apple tree and played golf for all they were worth. That tree was surrounded with the true atmosphere of golf. It is to be wondered why it has not been more firmly welded into the history of the game in this country. It should be a part of the great seal of the United States Golf Association. Maybe someday someone will immortalize it in some fashion or another, maybe a poem; but so long as we retain the true apple tree atmosphere around our clubs, it did not live in vain after all.

The San Francisco Golf and Country Club's stately clubhouse overlooks players and gallery at the eighteenth hole of the first round of the California State Women's Championship in 1931.

9 ORIGINALITY IN CONSTRUCTION

NOT LONG AGO I was amazed to hear a well-known golf constructor declare that there was but little that might be considered original in the golf construction of to-day. He asserted that our best holes were copies of time-honored and famous holes of British courses. Certainly I do not agree with him, and in my opinion some of these models which surely were grand holes a dozen years ago have completely lost caste since the introduction of far-flying balls.

Nevertheless, Great Britain provides us with some excellent types, even under present conditions, but attempts to copy them have produced holes of extreme mediocrity, and certainly a bit of originality would have been more effective. American courses fairly teem with Redans and Eden holes. A short time since when inspecting one of the latter type, I was reminded of a story.

A widow, accompanied by six children, visited the studio of a celebrated portrait painter. "We wish you to paint Father's picture," they chorused.

"Delighted," replied the artist, "bring the old gentleman around for a sitting."

"It can't be done," sniffled the widow, "he has been dead for ten years now. We haven't even got his photograph;—but we thought we might describe him to you."

And so, one after another they described minutely Father's features and general appearance. After some weeks the portrait was completed and the family lined up before the canvass and regarded it in wonder. There was depicted every described feature; nothing was lacking, but finally the good woman exclaimed, "Yes, that's Father all right;—but how changed he seems."

As I regarded that attempted reproduction of the famous old hole at St. Andrews there were features which were similar, but the hole looked about as much like the Eden Hole as the Eden Musee.

Every great golf hole possesses many natural features which collectively make it a great hole, each dovetailing with the others and without all of them there is something lacking which spoils the whole. It is not Nature's ensemble. So why not consider the material which Nature has given us to work with to the exclusion of any attempt to distort it to a sorry imitation.

On one occasion I was going over a course which I had planned. The green committee accompanied me, and finally we stopped by one of the finest natural greens it ever has been my good fortune to find. Imagine my consternation when one of the gentlemen suggested that here was offered a magnificent opportunity to duplicate a certain green on one of America's best known courses. The green which he mentioned is a remarkably fine one and, as a matter of fact, it could have been reproduced at this spot very easily, but to me it seemed like a sacrilege to think for an instant of ruining a wonderful natural creation in an attempt to copy. In my opinion the natural green was superior to the one which was mentioned, but I doubt if it would have approached its model in excellence had it been altered.

In some of the previous Golf Chats I think it was stated that the successful golf architect must be possessed of a big imagination. It takes imagination to create, but certainly none to copy. Redfern imagines and designs, and within six months his creations are copied by New York workshops. Do you suppose that one could not discriminate between the products when they passed on the Avenue? Maybe we men could not, but certainly the ladies could. I may be wrong, but I believe that the golfers of today want originality. Even those who are not particularly analytical sense the difference between a purely natural hole and one which suggests the artificial, and copied holes are artificial.

Without a doubt the most impressive natural golf hole which I have ever seen exists on a yet to be developed course at Ithaca, N. Y. When I discovered it I am sure the thought that it may have resembled to some extent one of the most famous golf holes in Great Britain never occurred to me. It was magnificent and alluring in itself. Afterward its similarity to the existing hole suggested itself and I am very sorry it did, for it may hamper its development along natural lines. A purely original treatment should develop a great golf hole, but as a copy I know that it would always appear to me as a rank imitation.

10   FORCED CONSTRUCTION

Figure One: Burying rock in a trench drain.

IT GOES WITHOUT SAYING that the ideal methods of golf course construction follow the natural lines of least resistance. Certainly they are the most economical. These "Naturals" are sought diligently by the successful architect, but frequently he is forced to connect them with a link that is quite artificial, no matter how natural it may be made to appear. This forced construction invariably is expensive as a unit but usually it makes for economy when the average cost is fixed.

The photograph (Figure One) was made recently and shows the hugest "Trench Drain" I ever have seen. While it functions as a drain, its greatest value is as a grave for the great rocks, dragged in for burial by tractors from the immediately adjoining area, which is being converted from virgin forest to fairway. To be sure, this particular stretch was far from ideal but it happens to be an

unavoidable connecting link and consequently necessary. This unit was costly but those rocks will never see the light of day again for they will "stay put." Work of this magnitude would have rather staggered us twenty-five years ago. Now it is a part of the day's work and we wade right into it when forced to it. Several years since, our construction work in Canada made it necessary to change the course of a good sized stream of water, which gloried in the name of river like a great ceremony for a small saint. But River or what-you-will, it was so located that a new channel was necessary before the course as a whole might be past criticism. As a matter of fact the actual cost was not nearly so much as the layman would anticipate. Such work seldom is. For example, the removal of timber is rather appalling for the layman to contemplate but modern methods and equipment keep costs down to moderate bounds and the actual work to astonishingly brief periods. But Rock, while not a problem, is another thing again and to ignore the costs of handling it is sheer folly. Yet golf must be played in sections were rock is in great evidence and construction is forced to meet the situations. The tacky method is common—a sort of semi-camouflage, hideous to behold and irritating to maintain. There is but one true way and that is to count the cost and if it is worth while, put it out of sight until it will take some finding.

The photographs (Figures Two and Three) illustrate a most interesting problem of forced construction. Figure Two shows a gentle hillside after tractors with scoops have been at work, cutting down the grade A as indicated by the dotted line. Above the line B shows top soil first removed from the entire area. The six foot man is walking along the cut and it is easy to see that fully four feet have been removed and used to fill a low area, which partially shows in the foreground. This is a vitally necessary connecting hole and as the entire construction was forced, the cost was greater than any three other holes of the course, as may be conceived after analyzing the work shown by the photographs. The hole has been made a dog-leg of drive and full mashie length. It was necessary to find our way

Figure Two: Top soil and cut of hill.

Figure Three: A drained swamp and ramp.

to the point directly under the arrow. Here the green was located at a point which naturally was not a place for a green at all. To make this point visible, the cut and fill as described was necessary. Before leaving this photograph let us concede that the top soil (B) has been replaced and some well rotted manure worked in. We have this much of our forced hole. Now for the other and even more important end (under the arrow as shown by Figure Three).

The line of play to this green is directly ahead as you regard the photograph. First a Cribbing of hewn logs was made, staunch in itself but backed by concrete, for this is to receive a fill of approximately three thousand yards of earth. A swamp has been drained, a Drag Line, operating between "Dead Men," has removed the muck over the ramp on the left for very necessary fill and a fine lake of clear water will guard the green on the front and right. Here is a fine example of super work of forced character. It yields a tough hole for par play but a safe route around

to the left, gives the conservative players every opportunity for his 5. The only hazard on the hole is the lake and yet the play for par is most exacting. This is an example of building holes without resort to unnecessary sand pits, an observation contained in another article and one which seems to have aroused considerable comment pro and con. But I am firmly convinced that most of our courses are over-bunkered.

The Winged Foot course has been awarded the National Open for 1929, and neither the East or the West course has added a trap since I planned them. Yet I believe the West Course, over which the championship will be played, to be a stern test of any man's golf exactly as it is, with comparatively few pits save those on the sides of the greens. These require long rifle-like seconds from the class players. Ordinarily the lower classes are playing their thirds into the same lanes, so what is the real difference?

11 FROM THE GROUND UP

The author rescued from a suck-hole.

A MAJORITY of the tracts of land selected for golf courses throughout America today present natural advantages—that is usually the reason for the selection. Easy undulations grading to gentle hills—lakes and running brooks—splendid groves of specimen trees—fine soil conditions—all these influence the choice of site, and very properly. But there are occasions when the builder of courses has none of these to his hand—when the ground stretches away in every direction to drab nothingness—*and sometimes there is no ground.* It is with the last condition that this article has to deal.

It is not given to all sections of this country, where the building of a course is a necessity, to have ideal conditions. The climate may be unfriendly, but various localities have learned the secrets of developing and keeping satisfactory turf under the most exasperating climate vagaries. But there are some God-forsaken expanses where man decides golf must be, and it is then the golf architect starts with nothing; yea, even less than nothing, for if there happened to be solid ground it would be something. Ground has to be made.

Several years ago, the writer was retained by the Stone & Webster Company of Boston to plan and advise in the building of a course over a swamp area, most of which was covered with water. The reclaiming of this swamp involved nothing new. It was the routine of establishing powerful dredges in a nearby channel, and pumping the bottom to fill the marshes. Every engineer has known of this model for years and can calculate the cost of reclaiming almost to a yard. But usually the fill is stopped at a safe, flat grade. If this was all, the builder of courses would have nothing more than a monotonous floor over which to step out into the various lengths of a collection of golf holes. Obviously the conception and construction of a course under these conditions are purely mechanical. There is about as much to inspire one as the eating of a waffle. The sitting down at a desk and the general orienting of the holes begins the work. There is to be said in its favor, however, style is uncramped and given free reign in arranging distances and sequences of shots, for thus far we are working through space. After this beginning, the architect makes his plan in detail, indicating the teeing-grounds, fairway, putting greens, hazards and, most necessarily to disguise the ugly foundation, an ambitious scheme of tree-planting and general landscaping. Now for the real work, which obviously must be from the ground up.

In the instance before us, I located an establishment where they made patterns for ornate work in cement, and working there with ordinary modeling clay, I modeled the entire course in sections, which fitted together perfectly when cast in plaster. This was accomplished easily by enlarging to a desired working scale, the original plans of

A filled-in mound after removal of forms.

How the mounds were built: Forms were erected and the river bottom pumped in.

one inch to a hundred feet. The flat scale of the model was one inch to twenty feet. With this model completed, I conferred with the company's engineers and various elevations were given them for additional fill. Every fairway was broken up into plateaus and various rough contours. Of course the sites for the greens were similarly treated, but the actual contouring of the fairway with natural-looking dunes in this artificial manner was a new trick. These huge, but gently sloping mounds had to look not only impressive when close at hand, but when hundreds of yards distant. Nearby they were gigantic, particularly in view of the fact that their size was enhanced by the general flatness of the surrounding filled land.

To make the additional fill over the areas indicated by the model, great forms of boards were constructed, sometimes to the heights of fifteen and twenty feet, and into these more harbor bottom was pumped. Then the forms were knocked down and moved to other points for similar use.

With this rough grading accomplished, there was something more to build on than at the start, but in reality we were only reaching the construction stage, where other courses start. Thereafter the process was not unusual. Contours were blended by means of scoops, although for a

time while the fill was finding itself the footing was frequently precarious. Once the architect permitted his two hundred pounds to sink ingloriously into a suck-hole or air pocket, which acted much like a quick-sand, and if sturdy aid had not been close at hand the consequences would have been much more alarming than well mucked underpinning. Just before this, at night, one of the workmen nearly lost his life before aid came to him in this same hole. Of course this danger and similar hazards were remedied.

Is the work at end now? Scarcely. As the fill is nearly pure silica the entire course has to be top-soiled, the fairway to a depth of four inches and a foot over every green. The hauling of all this material from a point nearly eight miles away constituted a detail of construction cost, which you may estimate if you are so minded. Certainly the building of a course under these conditions is costly, but I insist it is the only way to build impressively when you have nothing more with which to build.

When you have low flat land into which you cannot excavate with out hitting water the work must be from the ground up. If there is no scenery, it must be made. Where a round of golf ceases to be inspiring it ceases to be a pleasure.

12   WATER HAZARDS

The tenth on the beautiful Five Farms course of the Baltimore Country Club.

WHEN ground for a golf course is selected, the committee is rather sure to cast their eyes around in search of water. A natural lake is regarded as a gift of the gods, and any sort of running stream meets with approval. Sometimes this great desire for water hazards has influenced committees to such an extent, when several tracts of land were available, that the property upon which the water existed was selected in preference to another, which in every other respect was more suited to the game.

It is curious how water hazards, judiciously distributed to a reasonable extent, appeal to golfers. The same space might be occupied by sand-pits of grassed hollows, which would guard a green or punish wayward shots just as effectually, but the water is preferred in most instances. Often it is used too frequently and consequently the charm is lost because it is so common.

There are obvious reasons why water hazards appeal to green committees. When once established they take care of themselves. There is no sand to be hauled and cared for. When the banks once are smoothed until they meet the water in a natural fashion, they only have to be trimmed up occasionally and the cost of upkeep consequently is very little. The players like the water because it breaks the monotony of fairway extending over meadowland, hole after hole. It makes pleasant breaks in the course and generally the beauty of the surroundings pleases the eye. The fact remains that water on the course is highly popular.

Usually holes are constructed to fit in with water as it exists. Often enough the streams serve their duties admirably but there are times when they occur at spots which are not quite to the liking of the builder. As a matter of fact it is no great work to change the channel of a meadow or woodland stream. It only calls for the digging of a new one, the diverting of the water and the closing up of the original bed. There are many holes which could be helped amazingly by the switching of a stream.

The greatest criticism which may be found with water hazards as we find them generally concerns the conditions of their banks. Very often they are rank and filled with holes, from which it is impossible to extricate a ball at times. Committees should remember that there must be no spot on the course from which it is impossible to play, but this is overlooked to an almost criminal degree on many courses.

I am sure that I have never seen a water hazard which might be permitted to remain in exactly its natural state.

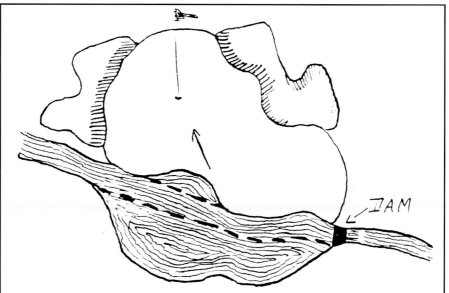

There always is something to be done. For the most part the meadow streams are too narrow, frequently so narrow that a ball must literally fall into it before staying there. It is an easy matter to widen the hazard by sloping the banks, and this slope should be extended well up into the fairway on the side where a ball enters the hazard. When the near banks are higher than those beyond there is a tendency for balls to hurdle the hazard. The widening of a water hazard always increases its efficiency and usually adds to its beauty. To illustrate this I have sketched a green and a guarding hazard of water, which has to be crossed in the direction of the arrow. Let us look at it for a moment.

It is to be conceived that the original stream ran in the channel, indicated by the dotted lines. To be sure that this old stream served its purpose to an extent, but by the construction of a small dam, the water has been allowed to overflow the original confines to the adjoining low ground and this miniature lake considerably improves the situation, both in its effectiveness and beauty. It is to be assumed that a slope from the fairway has made a natural basin here, but if it does not exist artificial banks may be built with little expense. It will be noticed, too, that a gentle inroad has been dug into the green itself to relieve a

rather formal line of the old water-course. The bank on the fairway side should be sloped naturally but in such a manner as to make it rather sure that any ball leaving the fairway shall find a resting place in the water. If it is permitted to remain rank the rough will stop many just penalties.

Sometimes entirely artificial lakes are encountered. They have been built possibly as reservoirs, into which water from a remote source is pumped to supply the necessities of the course. This is desirable, particularly when the water comes from springs and it is too cold to go to the turf. The raising of the temperature in a reservoir is necessary and at the same time the arrangement may be fitted into the lay-out to improve the demands of the course's play. But when these reservoirs are built, in nine times out of ten they are severely artificial in appearance. The outlines are mathematically precise. It would have been quite as easy to roughly curve the outlines and break up the bath-tub-like edges with natural-looking contours provided one had imagination. I think that the explanation of this may be found in an observation which was made to me several weeks ago by the chairman of a green committee of a club which had called me to make plans for a reconstructed course. He is a well known engineer and had been responsible for several of the existing holes. I found parallel holes and greens built in absolute regular lines without any relief. He said: "I guess that we engineers can think only in straight lines."

I have turned that remark over many times in mind and with it is driven home the conviction that the greatest fault of golf courses is that they have been conceived by straight-line thinkers, men who are fitted to the work in every respect other than following the lines of nature. The engineer must imagine nothing. He depends upon figures and drawings which must be exact to a small fraction.

Water hazards are popular and the builder of courses is glad enough to introduce them in his plans wherever he can, although it must be admitted that in some instances it is overdone. In the old days the

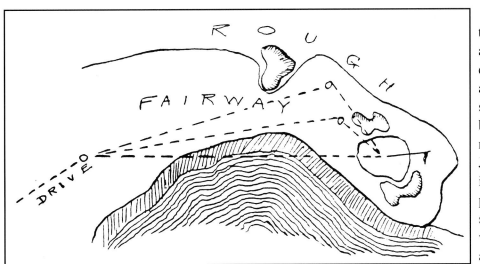

to the placement and length of the drive. The plan of a part of a two-shotter, which is being built on the new course at Port Jervis, New York, illustrates the point. The sketch shows the several ways to the green after a drive of

shots almost invariably were played directly across water, and frequently the modern plans give the player no alternative from making the carry or "getting the drink." However, there is the tendency to make the carries of water elective, with a decided advantage, of course, if the courageous shot over a portion of the hazard is accomplished successfully.

Our sketches from time to time have attempted to illustrate the importance of building holes in such a manner as to make the second shot bear a distinct relation

two hundred yards. The waters of a stream bound the fairway on the right and a diagonal carry to the green confronts the player, who may elect to get home with a long mid-iron or possibly a spoon. However, there is a safer route to the left, although the green cannot be reached unless a bit of the water hazard is carried or the tee-shot be of unusual length.

In the sketch the green is shown, opening its best face to the direct shot over the water.

The Island Green at Old York Country Club in 1914 (now known as Abington Club).

13 TREES AND THE COURSE BEAUTIFUL

IN THE WRITING of things which come under the consideration of those who build and maintain courses, there is not trouble in finding topics. The difficulty presents itself in the doing of justice to them. Frequently, the things which seem trivial to the rank and file of golf players are details that have been considered of so much importance as to cause great study by the course architect. Take trees for example. Possibly some splendid specimen has appealed to the architect to modify the plan of a hole rather than put ax to it and quite a little ingenuity has been exercised in consequence. Yet to those who afterward play the course day after day that tree supplies a charm even though some may be so lacking in an appreciation of nature as to be quite oblivious to its existence. To some, one tree is very like another. To others its influence is as satisfying as anything a round of golf may provide.

Certainly some of the most notable and charming courses have been constructed on land which was more or less heavily timbered. Naturally many trees have been removed in the process of building. When course construction was in its infancy the meadows were sought and few ever gave a thought about taking to the woods. As a consequence, the majority of courses laid out at that time were generally monotonous. After a time teeing grounds were placed among trees and later the fairway stretched through occasional wooded sections. Fine soil conditions exist in the woods and the cost of clearing is not great, particularly where the covering is small second growth. It may look desperate enough to the layman but an experienced constructor scarcely gives the clearing work a second thought. Usually the twisting of a fairway through timber brings to view prominently fine trees along the sides, which previously have been rather lost in a general tangle. And here may it be remarked that fairways should be rather irregular in shape and not like bowling-alleys extending through the woods.

Obviously there is considerable less work in opening a hole out from a wood than in ending one there. From the teeing ground the clearing gradually fans out. When playing in, there must be considerably more room for the finish of shots. And the greens may not be too closely adjacent to surrounding trees, for in the autumn the falling leaves are troublesome, and tree roots take to themselves considerable food and drink, which rightly belongs to the turf of the putting green. Poplars are particularly troublesome in both respects and frankly, I have but small regard for even the best behaved varieties of that family. There are trees and trees! Evergreens are the most desirable neighbors for the putting greens.

There may be still a few survivors of a once magnificent family, the chestnuts, but for the most part they are blighted and stretch out only dead and ghostly branches. Have no qualms about removing those unsightly skeletons to bring to view some sturdy hickory, elm, oak or a similarly shapely species which is inspiring to look upon. So must judgment be used in removing trees, to the end that every possible beauty be featured so long as it does not interfere with the sound play of the game. Certainly the necessity of lofting over a barrier of trees cannot be countenanced although this situation still exists in some sections of the country and naturally the courses are of antiquated design. But play through woods should not be overdone. It may be quite monotonous. Introduce just enough for variety.

As to the featuring of open play around woods, here usually is provided opportunities for dog-leg holes—a type which has done much to improve the plan of modern courses. The chance to feature prominently specimen trees is greater than in cutting directly through the heart of timber and it is highly desirable that an especially striking tree or group, should mark the turn of the play. The double dogleg, three shot-hole originated in the building of a hole along the side of a wooded tract. Whether play is directed through or along woods, the underbrush should be cleared thoroughly for a considerable distance off the fairway. It is quite enough to penalize a wayward shot by making the player get out without vexation and over-heavy punishment of a lost ball.

Trees can never be out of place nearby a teeing ground. They lend comfort to waits and rest, and if they are fine specimens a certain dignified individuality is added to the hole. On the new dual courses at Baltusrol the fairway of one hole was forced slightly by the architect in order to make possible the featuring of several magnificent, old horse-chestnuts for the next teeing-ground.

The Great Elm on the tenth hole of Winged Foot East.

Trees as a Setting to a Green at Rockwood: Situated on the Hudson, at Tarrytown, New York. Trees must, of course, be not so close as to shade a green and rob it of moisture, nor so thick as to shut off the currents of air. And trees need expert care and attention every bit as much as do greens and fairways.

TREES of the better sort, well shaped and really fine specimens, are admired and loved by a vast majority of people in all walks of life, everywhere. Those unfortunates, who remain cold and impassive in the presence of the nobles of the forest, have something wanting in their make-up something that would make them happier. I find one of the greatest joys of my profession in working among the trees, for I cannot conceive an inland course without them. Indeed, I like many. In my examinations of properties and estimating their worth as golf courses, my first reaction is to the natural terrain and soil conditions. Then immediately I turn my attention to the trees and brooks. How may the course be planned, after observing the vital elemental necessities, to bring forth prominently and impressively the best of the trees? The presence of numerous groves makes it not difficult to plan a beautiful course over rather flat and featureless ground, and whenever I am called upon to estimate the probable cost of constructing a course over territory which

is barren of trees, the figures must include the cost of tree planting, not because it is desirable only, but vitally necessary.

In cutting fairways through the forests, sometimes it is impossible to avoid the destruction of some fine trees, even though ingenuity has been taxed to swing away from some outstanding specimen. When this is unavoidable and the death warrant signed I confess to the weakness of being absent during the execution. But while this is necessary at times, it invariably is a fact that the cutting away of many worthless and less esteemed trees brings forth to view many good ones, which for years have been hidden away in a rowdy growth, unseen and unappreciated.

My usual procedure in clearing a fairway through the woods, after the presence of specimen trees has been noted and allowed for, is to confine the first removals to an area of fifty feet on each side of the center fairway line. In this way we remove only trees which obviously cannot remain and as the final clearing takes place, giving the fairway necessary width, it is much easier to shape the sides. This shaping of the sides is very important, as I hope my two sketches will illustrate. One shows the usual method of cutting through woods, an almost mathematically precise pattern, unpleasant to the eye because of its monotony. The proper cutting, illustrated by the companion sketch, shows an extremely irregular line on each side, and of course it follows that the presence of the finer trees more or less dictates that line. However, this cutting serves a purpose other than making the hole beautiful and free of the artificial. It adds greatly to its playing interest. For instance, see what happens to the sliced drive, which finds trees interfering with the second shot even though the tee shot has not ended in the woods but rather in the cleared bay of semi-rough. This, in a measure, is true in the case of the longer pulled drive. This plan permits of many variations, naturally suggested by the character of the trees themselves and the contour of the ground, for though we strive for artistic effect it must not be permitted to interfere with our conception of good golf nor introduce

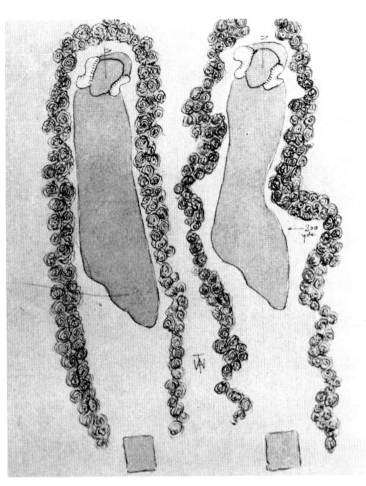

Fairways through the trees: One laid out artistically and designed for good golf as well as most pleasing to the eye; the other just a road cut straight from tee to green.

The fairway under construction on the Upper course at Baltusrol.

unjust penalties. Naturally this irregular cutting or clearing requires more space than does the more formal method, but how much more worthy it is. The significance of the cut-in clearing for the sliced drive was suggested to me a number of years since by the late Peter Lees, who was construction superintendent for me at the time.

Certainly the irregular clearing of trees deserves more than passing thought. Only too frequently are courses made hideous by the planting of long straight lines of nursery trees to separate parallel fairways. Poor scrawny things, each standing in naked isolation, they are unsightly and impotent. When it is necessary to do a bit of separating it is far more effective to group a few good trees at a point where they will do the most good, and surely the grouping is easier on the eyes.

A glance at my sketch will reveal the clearing of trees beyond the green. This is a good thing to do to insure a clear passage of air over the green, particularly if the trees are in the way of the prevailing breezes and winds. Greenkeepers know the value of ventilation of their greens. It keeps the Brown Patch down considerably and gives the turf some breathing, which is quite as necessary with the grass as among humans. Do not leave trees too near putting greens. A close proximity brings the roots to take the moisture from the turf. The previous photograph of Rockwood shows an entirely safe tree surrounding of a putting green.

In ending, let it be said that money spent on expert care of the club's fine trees is money well spent. If the budget must be cut, spare that set aside for the trees, even in these days of rigid economy: fine trees are only replaceable in the span of a lifetime.

Locating stakes for future fairways and greens: When the architect must become an engineer and use the surveyor's transit to lay out lines for construction.

Among the hundreds of golf courses that I have designed and constructed, Aldecress (now known as Alpine) was by far the toughest course to build that I ever encountered. At that time a coterie of very wealthy men desired me to prepare for them a course on this rocky tract in close proximity to the Palisades of the Hudson. There was a deal of tree removal (big fellows) draining and above all, very far above all, we were messing around in huge stone outcrop over the entire area.

46

The Duel Hole—San Francisco Golf and Country Club.

SOME years ago I was planning a course on the American side of the Niagara River. Observing the faint but still distinguishable lines of a trench, I was curious enough to make inquiries concerning it. Few could tell me much about it until finally I was handed over to one of the oldest inhabitants of the section and he informed me that it was a part of the redoubt thrown up by Colonial troops during the Revolutionary War. Probably, had I remained longer, someone else, better versed in history, might have unfolded some mighty interesting facts

about this old breastwork. It did not occur to me at the time to press my queries, but some years afterwards it did, when other relics turned up now and again on other ground on which golf courses were built. Indian remains were and are not uncommon. Out in Ohio there is a certain course constructed all about well defined Indian mound-work of unusual significance and interest. Sometime I must delve into the history of it. Recently on the course of the Mexico City Country Club, president Harry Wright showed me many bullet marks on the clubhouse walls, dating from the

Obregon fights and further he showed me the part of the course where this general had his battle lines.

Now it came to pass some years ago that I was called to California to plan the reconstruction of the course of the San Francisco Golf and Country Club, at Ingleside. The present course is the result of that visit, and at the time I acceded to the request of Roger Lapham to remain for a few days longer than had been anticipated, for the purpose of personally contouring several of the new greens. Of these, the seventh, was of peculiar interest, a one-shotter, a full iron to a green in the valley below. This, most appropriately, is called the Duel Hole, for here in the year 1859, the last formal duel in the United States was fought, between U. S. Senator David C. Broderick, of California, and Supreme Court Judge David S. Terry. Broderick was adverse to dueling but recognized the necessity of accepting the challenge as a man of honor, fearing that his political friends particularly would charge him with cowardice if he declined. He was shot dead. The two monuments indicate that the duelists stood about ten paces apart, a short range and deadly.

As the green took form, I had looked over at the little flat from time to time, and the scene on a morning, seventy years before, pictured itself in mind. Those slopes had afforded an admirable point of vantage for the spectators, who had driven out to the spot from the young town of San Francisco. Most likely it was soon after sun-up with the early morning air charged with the electricity of dramatic situation, which must be followed by tragedy. Then the arrival of the principals, their seconds and the surgeon; the formalities, and two men facing each other

The two monuments mark the positions of the duelists.

with pistols, awaiting the signal to fire. Then the roar of the guns, echoing along the ravine and the hills on either side, as the morning breeze cleared the smoke, revealing one man standing erect looking across the ten paces where his fallen adversary's life was going out to the rising sun, over the hills, red with poppies.

And now golfers troop by, match after match, day after day. I wonder if anyone ever thinks at all about the two Davids? Probably not, for life must go on.

When we built the course at Aldecress, in Bergen County of northern New Jersey, there came to my observation a relic of Revolutionary days. Close by the Aldecress course runs the old Closter Dock Road, and it was along this highway that General Howe led his British forces toward Trenton after crossing the Hudson. Evidently he must have tarried here for a while, at least sufficiently long to execute two patriots. On the lane, which leads to the first teeing ground of Aldecress, is the stone foundation of an old building. There had stood the Closter grist mill of the "Patriot Miller Demarest." On the 11th of May, 1779, the mill was burned by Howe's troops and the miller's two sons, Cornelius and Hancomb, were shot by a firing squad.

This all provides background, color. Only recently, on the course at Barnton, near Edinburgh, the greenkeeper unearthed a stone slab, two feet beneath the surface. It covered a grave of the Bronze Age, antiquarians putting the date not later than 1000 B.C. For three thousand years that ancient grave had been hidden from mortal eyes until the greenkeeper's work on the golf course disclosed it.

WITHOUT a doubt one of the most certain earmarks of a modern golf course are twisting, irregular shaped fairways.

The boy from the backwoods shows unmistakably by the cut of his hair that Mother has taken the sugar bowl, placed it helmet-like over his head, and cropped around the rim. Whenever you see a fairway cut with the same precision, you may know immediately that the green committee is composed of antiquarians who are "sot in their ways."

In a moment I shall discuss the simple twisting of the fairways of comparatively straight holes, but at this time let us consider the extreme types where the fairways snake around Dog-legs and Elbows.

As a rule, the two terms are used indiscriminately, but I always have made this distinction. A Dog-leg hole provides some pronounced obstruction, which forms a corner in a twisted fairway from either side. If it be impossible to carry over this obstruction, but at the same time necessary to get beyond it in order to open up the next shot, we have a Dog-leg.

If a similar obstruction may be carried by a courageous shot, which is rewarded by a very distinct advantage, we have an Elbow.

There is still a third variation, where a corner is formed close by the green itself, usually by the encroachment of a hillside or sandy waste, and this type is known as a Cape hole.

The inclusion of these very twisted types lends variety to any course, and in a great measure they may eliminate the old evil of paralleling which is encountered so frequently on courses of common pattern. Then, too, these types require less bunkering than the straight-aways, for usually the projecting areas are provided by nature. In laying out courses inland where wooded sections are numerous, the planning of the Dog-leg is quite simple. The trees are permitted to remain along the side for such a distance as may be considered proper for a well-hit shot to exceed. Of course, the length of this shot would be regulated by the slopes of the fairway and the character of the turf.

Under normal conditions, a player should be required to drive at least two hundred yards before the barrier to his second shot is removed. From this point the fairway turns abruptly either to the right or left, opening up the green or its approaches. The first hole of the new course at Pine Valley provides an excellent example of the Dog-leg, and, indeed, many of our most modern courses present equally admirable types.

Last year I was called to Wernersville, Pa., to reconstruct a nine-hole course, and my rough sketch illustrates one of the new holes. Inasmuch as the corner of the swamp at Wernersville may be carried to a distinct advantage, It should be designated as an Elbow.

While the length is well within the command of a drive and a mid-iron or mashie, the player who declines to attempt the hazardous carry of the swamp will find it exceedingly difficult to reach the green with a second, for the bunkering is very close.

49

The word Rough, which looms forth threateningly from the sketch, need not carry terror with it. I insist that rough country should be a prominent feature on every course, but I am no believer in the matted rank grass variety, where balls are rather sure to be lost, and vexatious, irritating delays occasioned. Like the instruments of torture from the days of the Inquisition, this form of rough belongs to golf of the past.

Rough country may be created to exact its penalty of one stroke without having the lost ball plague lurking within its borders.

Twisted fairways offer other inducements than the mere introduction of encroaching areas of hazard or rough, which may be carried to distinct advantage. It provides a remedy for the great and ancient evils, parallel holes.

Scarcely a course, built a dozen years ago, was without parallels. Side by side they stretched, with a meager strip of rough between, which caught the ball which was slightly off line but useless in hindering the very wild player from gaining a pleasing lie on the fairway beyond. From here he usually was quite as likely to find the green with his second shot as his straight down-the-alley opponent.

The designers of old time courses either closed their eyes to the evil or else were powerless to find a remedy. It is so easy to fit the holes in parallel lines, particularly when one has to lay out a tract which is nearly square. This treatment requires no more brain-fag than marking off a tennis-court. It was not golf, but it was the best they knew only a few years since.

I well remember the remark of one of the Oxford-Cambridge golfers who visited America with Mr. John Low. He had been asked his opinion of a certain then prominent course. Looking out on the parallels, he smiled sadly but evaded a direct reply to the enthusiastic green

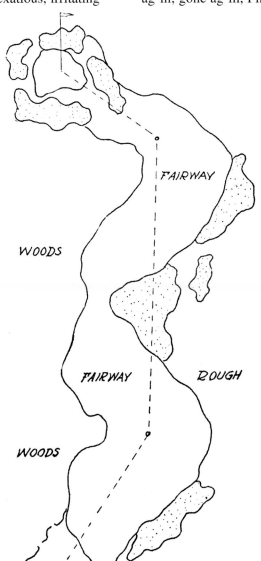

Double Dog-Leg Hole.

committeeman at his side, but when the latter had departed, Hunter (it was Norman Hunter) turned to me and said:

"It reminds me of that bit of doggerel, 'In ag'in; out ag'in; gone ag'in, Finnegan.'"

But back to the twisting fairways. I never have seen a case of "parallelitis" which could not be helped by the simple expedient of cutting the fairways irregularly. To be sure, some patients are beyond cure, but their condition may be relieved in a measure.

As an example of a very twisted fairway, let me offer a sketch of a three-shot hole. The three-shot hole is one of the most trying which the architect has to consider, for probably there are comparatively more thoroughly bad three-shot holes than those of any other type. Some seem to labor under the impression that a three-shot hole calls for nothing but brawn, and consequently ridiculously long holes of six hundred yards and over are to be found. As a matter of fact, the green of the three-shot hole should be small and very closely guarded, for it must be conceived that a long drive has been followed by an almost equally long and well placed brassey or cleek in order that the flag, which is beyond the range of any two shots, should be sought by an accurate mid-iron or mashie. In order that the player who had missed or half-hit either his drive or second shot, must be made to find himself out of the range of the green, a great hazard finds its way across the fairway, and this hazard should be anywhere from fifty to one hundred yards wide, for the reason already stated. If the far brink of this hazard is a trifle over four hundred yards from the teeing ground, two strong shots will carry it and permit the player to pitch to the green, which, let us say, is five hundred and twenty-five yards in all. Obviously, the great area of the hazard will not permit the player who was short of it in two, to reach home with his third, and it must be remembered, too, that the green itself is very small and too closely guarded to permit of its being held by a very long stroke.

The three-shot hole illustrated is quite original with the writer, and if there is another like it, I surely have never heard of it. The scheme provides a double dog-leg with a closely guarded green which cannot be seen unless two very long shots open it up. It is likely that further explanation is unnecessary, for the sketch, rough as it is, shows the problem.

It may seem curious that early American golf courses were laid out on such puny scales and along such unintelligent lines. The game was biff and bang, with little else to think of; no problems to solve. But, after all, it is not so much to be wondered at. Our early players were faddists whose conceptions of golf were exceedingly crude. How could they be expected to appreciate the finer points of the game as did those in the old country, where golf had been played for so many years?

For a long time the greatest obstacle in the way of modern courses in America was the opposition of the mediocre player. He fancied that any attempt to stiffen the courses must make them so difficult that the play would be beyond his powers. But now he realizes that the modern golf architect is keeping him and his limitations in mind all the while he is cunningly planning problems which require the expert to display his greatest skill in negotiating holes in par figures.

Where champions congregate: The testing links of the Shawnee C.C. on the banks of the Delaware.

I PRESENT a rough sketch showing three instances of the same shot to a green situated on a knoll, which stands out against the skyline. In each of the three examples there exists a different condition. In the first, a solitary tree stands on the slope to the left of the line of play but near the green. The second represents a tree beyond the green and the branches of which may be seen from the teeing ground (provided the hole is a short one), or from the point from which the shot to the green is played if it be an approach. The third shows only a green without any tree at all, nothing but the flag standing out in bold relief.

Although a great lover of trees myself, and reluctant to

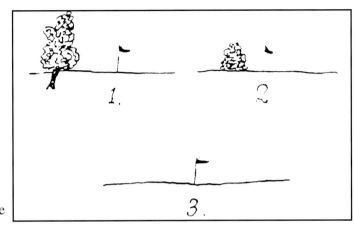

put the axe to a fine specimen which stands out prominently and beautifully, yet I do so frequently if the tree in question affects the play to any hole. And there is no doubt that a solitary tree, standing near the vicinity of a green, particularly one which is played with an iron and consequently demanding nice calculation, renders the judgment of distance very easy. Our eyes, accustomed to the sight of many trees, rather accustom themselves to distances when one tree stands out prominently as a guide. This is the best explanation I can offer. Without a doubt many may advance more subtle reasons, but the fact remains—a lone tree, standing near the end of a shot, makes the distance

The tenth hole of the Upper course at Baltusrol.

much easier to gauge, particularly if it be in full view as in Figure One.

One of the most difficult shots to any green is the second to the seventeenth hole at Pine Valley. It is difficult because the green stands out boldly against the sky and the shot appears to be much longer than it is in reality.

Some of the most attractive holes have been made through wooded tracts, but with many trees on either side of the fairway the guiding virtues of solitary trees is not in evidence. Still there can be no denying the effect of tree groups in distance estimates. The sixteenth on the course of the Somerset Hills Country Club, near Bernardsville, NJ, is called "Deception," and certainly it is one of the most deceiving holes imaginable. From teeing ground to green there are woods along the sides, and consequently the shot seems much greater than a mid-iron length. It is likely, though, that the deception of this particular hole is

made greater by reason of a winding stream, which was cunningly introduced.

One of the new courses at Baltusrol furnished a splendid example of the greatly changed aspect of a shot through the removal of several prominent trees close by the green. The hole in question is the tenth on the new Upper Course. The green is situated upon the top of a knoll and the line of play is slightly across the slope. When the several trees were removed, particularly one old wild-cherry, the distance immediately appeared longer than the iron-length, which it is.

On sea-side courses, where trees are few, my point is illustrated best. Here a single tree near a green catches the eye immediately, and as a consequence the player drops his shot with far more confidence and accuracy than he would were the surroundings severely rugged and unadorned.

Deception—the sixteenth hole at Somerset Hills.

18   TREES ON THE GOLF COURSE

The seventeenth hole at Rockwood Hall Country Club: At Tarrytown, N.Y., the home of the late Mr. William Rockefeller, looking over the glorious Hudson River. Possessing many magnificent trees, the Club took great care to preserve every one that it could in the design and construction of its golf course.

THE late Mr. Walter J. Travis frequently voiced the opinion that no tree had any place on a golf course. This expression of his view came during the days when he was solely a player. For a few years before his death, Mr. Travis engaged professionally in golf architecture and evidently he changed his opinion; converted or grudgingly tolerant he never said it in my hearing. But the fact that he did change is evinced by some of his work. This could not well be otherwise for the builder of courses is being forced more and more to take to timber, whether he likes it or not. I am free to confess my liking for it, a love of fine trees, which possibly should be entirely foreign to the natural instincts of a descendant of sailormen of a bleak New England coast. Yet, after all this is not so strange, for most people like trees, and long experience tells me, too, that they do like them on the golf course.

In building courses over a wide area such as spreads itself from the Atlantic to the Pacific oceans, I have found that the selected sites usually include a goodly acreage of woods. Near the sea, of course, the trees are characteristically stunted and scraggy, but even here they lend considerable charm in their rugged fashion. However, it must be borne in mind that the inland courses of America are in overwhelming majority and it is to the fine specimen trees, peculiar to the various localities, that we may for a moment direct our thought. Whenever one of the fine old fellows rears his branches in solitary splendor it immediately occurs to the architect that here is something that needs nothing except a whole lot of letting alone. If the contours of the surrounding terrain are fortunate, a putting green, not too remote from this sentinel, must contribute to the distinction and charm of the hole. A notable example of this is the great wine glass elm off the left rear of the second green of Winged Foot's West course. Not only is the tree impressive, but it marks the true line of play all the way from the teeing ground. In this fashion, outstanding trees may be used advantageously in designing a hole, to chart the channel, so to speak. This function of a tree suggests a point which is open to debate.

May not a solitary tree in some instance detract from the value of a hole in a measure? For example, in the case of a green played directly beyond the slope of a hillock and sharply defined against the sky. Barren of any nearby object, such as a tree for instance, the distance of the shot to the green is much more difficult to judge with accuracy than it would were there a tree or two standing forth

Chandler Egan in the 1904 Amateur at Baltusrol.

against the sky at the crest. All players of ability will bear witness to the baffling length to a naked green, but few actually realize how much more readily the estimate of the eye would be flashed to the brain if sight should fall simultaneously on a lone tree and its neighboring green. This is true beyond question and it suggests the query as to the true sporting limit of camouflage to make the shot unusually difficult to gauge or contrarily the extent of helpful influence to make it easy, or easier. While the point is somewhat of a digression from trees actually, it is open to discussion. But the placement of any tree, so close to the finish of a shot to the green that it may catch the ball and deflect it to a fortunate or unfortunate finish, cannot be condoned.

Forgive another digression in a rather sketchy article, but there are those who have found some humor in it. At the time, I did not, for the incident is personal. More than twenty years ago, Mr. Chandler Egan won the championship of the United States at Baltusrol. I played him in the first round of that tournament and at the end of

the eleventh enjoyed a lead of one hole. After our drives to the twelfth it looked for a brief moment as though my lead might go to two for my ball rested in the fairway within a short pitch to the green, while Mr. Egan had unleashed an unholy hook into a real jungle. How he ever got a club to that ball, or what manner of club it was, matters not, but that ball came out plenty. It would have continued its mad flight for a lot more than the player had hoped had it not come in violent contact with a lone tree, which grew immediately by the side of the green for no good purpose. After sampling nearly every branch of that tree for a good place to alight, the ball finally decided on a nice spot on the green itself very close to the cup. The birdie 3 evened the match which had looked like two down a moment before. In memory that tree was coupled

The twelfth green of the "Old Course" at Baltusrol.

with one of my life's darkest moments. Some years later, I had been retained by Baltusrol to remodel the course and extend it to its present thirty-six holes. One day the late Mr. Louis Keller, then of the Green Committee, heard the sound of axes eating into a half dead tree and hurried over to investigate. Nearby he found their golf architect looking on and smiling contentedly as he stood on the old twelfth green.

Now back to good trees again. I find that every committee has tree lovers in the majority and they do not hesitate to state their fears of certain holes which would seem to destroy sylvan beauty. It is easy to understand their abhorrence of tree removal. It has been mentioned already that every effort is directed to the swinging of holes, not only to save fine specimen trees and small groups, but to make them serve a definite purpose in the playing of the game. But often we find a large copse or a thick forest which must be penetrated. Those who grieve because of this necessity do not realize fully that opening up the fairway will not be a program of indiscriminate destruction but rather a painstaking effort to cut through in such a manner as to bring to view the best trees which long have been hidden away among unlovely companions. Woods are like communities and trees are like men. In each there are a lot of common nuisances and parasites that are best out of the picture altogether. In every forest you will find some rare old trees, oaks and elms, sycamores and hickories that have been hidden away from sight for many years with a tangle of non-descripts all about them. These we save, of course, as much as possible, but there are times when some truly grand trees have to go and it is not without a pang at their passing. This was particularly true in building the Municipal course of San Antonio, Texas. The Brackenridge Park tract contained slightly less than one hundred acres for golf purposes and it did hurt to see some of the magnificent pecan trees that had to be removed of necessity. There were many left standing, however. Here was an example of the value of trees when working over a restricted area. Had it not been for the covering of mesquite and huisache trees, which now divide the fairways and guard against danger, the building of the course on such a small acreage would not have been possible.

It must be admitted that during the weeks of the Fall, when trees are dropping their leaves, the sylvan greens are rather a care, but after all it means only a concentration of labor for a period and the charm of such greens surely is worth it. Wherever possible it is well to have evergreens close by the putting areas. I must confess a weakness for an occasional green or teeing ground among birches. But there is a warning to be given to the builders of greens in the woods. Be sure that avenues for air are provided. Unless the air is given a chance to circulate, with cuttings to the directions of the prevailing winds, the turf is very likely to suffer from the brown patch and smothering ailments. So much for greens among the trees.

Teeing grounds may just as well be beautifully located as not. Here is born every new hope in a round of golf. No matter how distressing has been the hole just finished fresh determination surges as foot falls on the next teeing ground. Why not let men get determined in comfort? An honest old tree can be very sympathetic and comforting if the golfer will take the time to look into its serenely complacent face and feel that way about it. It may be another weakness, but I do like to find such settings for teeing grounds. Possibly it is an inviting group, maybe a lordly, towering centenarian which still lifts an exalted and glorious head. I have known it to be an old apple tree, long since beyond the bearing of fruit, but offering a sturdy trunk about which a circular bench may be built whereon one may relax awhile.

The sixteenth at the Lakewood Country Club, a 100 yard shot over water.

56

The eighth hole on the "Old Course" at Baltusrol went directly up hill.

BACK in the '90's, when young courses of America were finding life, there were heard in all quarters this expression: "Sporty holes." For the most part, sporty holes called for shots across ravines or from one hill-top to another. Often they dropped from hills to greens far below, which feature frequently was not bad at all, but just as often they sported from valleys bang up-hill, which was very bad because the greens were necessarily semi-blind or totally so, but worse because they were extremely arduous to play. There were some holes so steep that golfers might not be too severely blamed had they attempted the ascent with Alpine stocks and yodeling while breath lasted. A big, woolly dog such as the pious monks of St. Bernard were wont to turn loose in the mountains with small casks attached, would not have been such a bad idea either, waiting with first aid at each summit green. Yet for years golfers toiled over these climbs, trying to make shots while puffing violently, their starting eyes half seeing the ball as they struck. Fortunately the years have seen the gradual passing of these back-breakers, although they are still to be encountered here and there. Certainly no worthy builder of modern courses will conceive a hole directly up-hill if there is any way to avoid it. In working from one level to another it is a good rule to look for the longest way up and the quickest way down, and by the longest way up, I mean the least arduous with the old-time cow-path as an example.

Several years ago, however, I was guilty of building one although the fault was not mine. Eighteen very satisfactory holes were planned and nearly constructed when some adjoining property, which had been considered available until the work had gone ahead too far to abandon or change, was suddenly snatched away because of the owner's change of heart and instead of an easy ascent through a swale, dog-legging to the higher level, the direct shot up-hill was the only alternative. Happily this may be only temporary, for it is hoped that the original line may still be followed eventually. But that hole has been a canker in the flesh and has troubled me more than I care to admit. This incident is introduced only to show how loathsome the up-hill hole is in my sight. This must not be confused with the fairway which is slightly up-grade nor that which presents a pronounced elevation which may be carried to gain the reward of good going beyond. It is the uninspiring slog, all carry, into the long hill that is so objectionable.

The old course of the '90's did not offend us then as

now. During the years we have gradually become accustomed to better holes over less violent topography, and when we do chance to encounter one of the hill-billies of other days, it comes as a bit of shock. I may make reference now to one that could not be criticized so freely not so very long ago. The old course of the Baltimore Country Club in Roland Park presented some pretty stiff hill holes. The first drive seemed to take one right off the roof of the world, and the last one was a tough grind up-hill, particularly punishing on a hot day. There were others, too, equally arduous. I was retained by the club to plan the new eighteen on the Oliver place, now known as Five Farms. There was no reason whatever for any comment or criticism of the Roland Park hill holes and none was volunteered. Yet I heard a number of the old members praising the course they had played for so many years, with never a complaint about the climbs. The new course was some distance away, and few had gone over the property. As the work progressed, some of these very men talked with me and the burden of their inquiries was invariably hill climbing. They wanted to be assured that the new holes would be somewhat less arduous.

It stands to reason that in some parts of the country, hills may not be avoided entirely, but as a rule this sort of land does not run into a great deal of money and it is only a question of using more acreage than usual, for it is easy to avoid the tough spots if there is room to get around them. Now, getting around the stiff slopes does not require great judgment in the placement of the teeing grounds, and this is the real solution of the breaking fairway problem. Avoid directing shots in any direction other than into the side that breaks. For example, if the fairway shows a rather pronounced slope from the right side, the teeing ground must be placed well to the left, and vice versa. The reason for this is quite obvious to any man that plays much golf. Playing into the slope straightens a ball out and it will not go racing away with the throw of the ground as it would if played directly along the slope, or worse still, with it. This naturally makes it necessary to provide wider fairway if the ground slopes from one side or the other. Often the grading of parts of the fairway, to offer a check against the ball moving fast from the natural side slope, is necessary. This cutting and filling in zones is not expensive work unless quantities of rock are encountered.

If the work is pursued intelligently, the slopes of hills may be cut away, twisted and turned and graded to a most satisfying fairway, approach or green. One thing must be guarded against however—wash. From the upper slopes, surface water will run down to gutter new earth and wash away top-soil and young grass. This must be prevented by ditching above and carrying the water away where it can make off without damage. And when it comes to building greens and their approaches into side slopes, it is well to work over a great area in order to have sufficient space to give long slopes to your contours, that the work, artificial as it has to be, may appear natural and pleasing, and not, like a railroad embankment, an offense to the eye.

The fourth green at Cedar Crest, Dallas—Clubhouse in distance. An examination of the picture of the green with a magnifying glass will show that it looks very difficult to hold and is likely to play havoc with some scores. The safe place to play for seems to be the back of the green.

58

20 THE OBLIQUE IN GOLF DESIGN

THE greatest difference in golf holes of the present and those of twenty-five years ago undoubtedly is the extending of the line of play across oblique lines rather than those at right angles. This simple principle, with elaborations which permit holes to be played in numerous ways, introduced elective play and finesse that was entirely absent before. Hazards built in echelon and greens opening up diagonally to a straight line from the teeing grounds, make the true line play something other than indifferent hitting straight ahead, sauce for goose and gander alike. In brief, the oblique lines make it possible for every class of player to extend shots only to the limitations of power, thus making it easier for the duffer to enjoy golf more, but at the same time calling for greater effort for the scoring of par and "birdies" than in the times when carries were obligatory and greens were faced at right angles and accepting, without great favor, shots from either side of the fairway.

The sketch illustrates the principle in a simple way. The green faces the left side of the fairway and its length and contour greatly favor the second shot from that side, which can only be gained by a courageous carry of the diagonal

hazard at the longest range. The drive that has electively carried midway finds a much more difficult second to get home, while the timid drive that declines the carry altogether leaves a truly improbable shot to the green and one which suggests cautious safety play to the green's entrance. Naturally such a hole demands more than the usual observation of wind conditions when the markers on the teeing ground are placed for the day. It will require but a little imagination, as the sketch is studied, to see all the diagonals pulled around to right angles in the mind's eye. Then we would have a hole of the old type with the driving hazard directly across the fairway, presenting precisely the same carry to champion and duffer, and the green offering no reward to the placed drive. As a matter of fact the large hazard area might be dispensed with altogether and there would still remain a tremendous advantage to the drive placed on the left of the fairway, provided the green was properly contoured and pointed obliquely as in the sketch. There is nothing new about all this for the arrangement has found place generally on all first-class courses for a long time now. However, it illustrates my answer to a question as the greatest

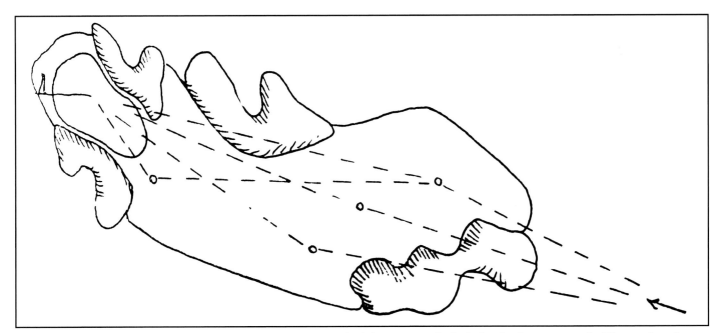

An interesting use of oblique design: A well-placed drive to the left opens up the hole for the long approach. The weaker player, keeping to the right, avoids an impossible carry and must place his second to the left to reach the green in three on a five hole equally interesting to him.

difference between modern courses and those of a quarter century gone by.

Now for the consideration of another point. Some years ago, Archie Compston asked me what I considered the ideal length for a one-shot hole and the limit of the yardage for this type. He quite agreed with my first reply, 185 yards, but he insisted that the one-shotter should not exceed 200 yards. This estimate of his limitation of yardage is right enough in my opinion if we assume that the hole

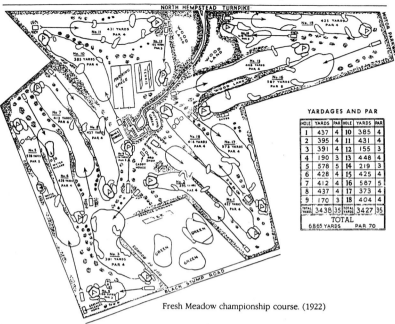

Fresh Meadow championship course. (1922)

HOLE	YARDS	PAR	HOLE	YARDS	PAR
1	437	4	10	385	4
2	395	4	11	431	4
3	391	4	12	155	3
4	190	3	13	448	4
5	578	5	14	219	3
6	428	4	15	425	4
7	412	4	16	587	5
8	437	4	17	373	4
9	170	3	18	404	4
TOTAL YARDS	3438	35	TOTAL YARDS	3427	35

YARDAGES AND PAR

TOTAL
6865 YARDS   PAR 70

with wood, other than spoon, is a drab affair and too long to be really interesting. Figuring four one-shot holes in a round, we have fourteen where we can step on the teeing ground and give full swing to the long wood, and as our well-designed courses call for placement as well as power, it is just as well to

has a normal playing length of 200 yards, but must we not really measure our holes by the rule of its playing length rather than its actual yardage as shown by the chain? It is quite easy to conceive of a hole that measures up to 225 yards or even 240, which is the accepted maximum yardage of the par 3, that would call for only a medium iron because of favoring terrain in front of the green, an elevated teeing ground or abnormal condition of turf. But I do think that any one-shooter that calls for a full stroke

limit the par 3's to very accurately hit irons. Certainly many of our courses are carrying their lengths to extremes that rob them of considerable interest on all occasions other than the comparatively infrequent meeting of giants. Under normal conditions, 6,500 yards should be quite enough to satisfy everyone on all occasions. I have said before, and repeat it here, that I believe many of the courses are extreme in length, extreme in putting areas and over bunkered through the fairway.

No. 1 Center Course, Ridgewood Country Club. This is a dog leg to the left across the lake. The carry straight over water is about 190 yards.

60

21 SEVERAL PATHS TO THE GREEN

THAT HOLES, which present several paths from teeing ground to green, meet with general approval is proved by the requests that committees provide more of them. They are demanded by the scratch players because their carrying powers will enable them to pick up distance to such a marked degree that ordinary opponents have but little chance of securing a half in par figures unless through extraordinary effort. Golfers of varying ability, grading all the way down to the duffer, like this type of hole, too, because it allows them to select an easier route than the one taken by others of greater skill and strength.

The hole illustrated shows several ways to the green of a two-shotter. The green is guarded well to protect it against inaccurately hit iron strokes. On the right and left are pits and the green slopes down to meet an arm of fairway on the right. On the left there is a distinct hummock, which melts into the green but at the same time deflects wayward shots into the hazards unless the shot is pitched with precision. In front, a large pit eats into the face of the green and this has to be carried if par figures are to be expected. A great area of barren quality stretches along the fairway on the left and out in front of the front pit.

Now it must be assumed that because this is designated as "rough" that it must be rank rough. I am not kindly disposed to long, closely matted growths in which balls are constantly lost to the utter discouragement and irritation of golfers who take to the links for pleasure and relaxation from business. Tufts of grasses, which clump from stools, with sand, gravel or the like between, make ideal rough where balls may be found with no great effort if marked down by players and caddies, but which is sufficiently rough to prevent great distance on the recovery. In the case of this hole it is to be assumed that the country along

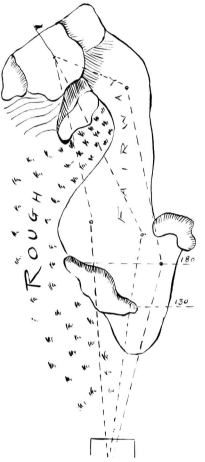

the left is forbidding enough to be respected and avoided.

The great driving pit on the left presents a graded carry and the long player who successfully negotiates the carry from one hundred and eighty to one hundred and ninety yards is left with a fairly easy jigger or half-iron over the easiest part of the front pit with the slope on the left of the green helping him considerably. The drive, which carries only one hundred and thirty to one hundred and sixty yards leaves a much more difficult approach of full iron length. But there remains a way to the right, around the pit, by which the short hitter may decline any carry at all, yet taking care that he does not go far enough to reach the pit on the right. From this point he may either take a chance of reaching and holding the green with a long spoon or brassey if the situation is desperate enough to warrant the effort, or else play safely along the fairway to the right, pitching on with his third.

This hole is being built on the new Texas course, Brook Hollow, at Dallas. The soil is very different from the "black land" of the white rock so common in the state, being of sandy loam composition with a sub-strata of clay.

Where the hole is being built there is a considerable stretch of "blow-sand," which will take the place of the rough area on the drawing, and it is an ideal condition.

Frequently in many sections these stretches of sand are to be found, and it is better to plan the fairway in such a manner as to use them as hazards; not that they cannot be grassed satisfactorily, but because very impressive hazards may be introduced with but little effort and cost. In front of the new home hole at Norwood, on the New Jersey coast, a stretch of drifted sand was used at no cost and the barren area goes a long way to make the hole distinctive.

22   FEATURING PUTTING GREENS

The greens at North Shore have fine bold undulating contours. Here Walter Hagen strokes a putt during the 1919 Met Open.

THERE are people whom we may meet casually whom we forget after going our respective ways, for there has been nothing about them which leaves even the faintest impression behind. We may look into their faces and vaguely recognize a general type; then we promptly forget the face and the man.

Sometimes in the passing crowd our eyes rest for a moment on a strange face, so strong, finely chiseled and so filled with character that although it is gone in a second our fleeting glance has indelibly stamped the features upon our memory.

Now, we are chatting on golf and not faces, but there is a parallel. A putting green has features just like a human, or, at least, it should have to be worthy of the name. Of course, there are many which are no more impressive than the vacant, cow-like expression of some people, but then again there are some with rugged profiles which loom head and shoulders above the common herd, and the moment we clap eyes on one of these, impulsively we murmur, "Ah! there's a green for you!"

The character of the putting greens and their approaches mark the quality of a course to a far greater extent than anything else. No matter how excellent may be the distances; how cunningly placed the hazards, or how carefully considered has been the distribution of shots,—if the greens themselves do not stand forth impressively the course itself can never be notable.

The best players will tell you that they like to play to a green that stands well up in the back. This is not a new observation, and yet the country is fairly cluttered with symmetrical, "pancakey" greens, which slope away from the line of play in a most brazen manner. They are utterly worthless and heartily cursed by every true golfer, and yet, strange to say, a great many similar putting greens are being built today. Such ignorance is inexcusable.

Naturally, those greens which are to be gained by lofted shots from iron clubs should slope more into the shots than those which, under ordinary conditions, are reached by the finish of balls running from wood. The irons are designed to impart underspin or "stop," and unless the green faces properly this spin cannot become effective. No matter how crisply played by master hands, a ball falling upon a receding green can get no bite. So our first step toward supplying our putting greens with character is the consideration of the type of shot which is to find that green and construct with that thought ever uppermost.

Nothing can supply a green with more character than bold undulations, and nothing can make a green more ridiculous-looking, than puny little kinks which some will insist are undulations. The long, gentle slopes make putting a fine art, and as the cups are changed from day to day, variety is introduced and the rounds are never monotonous. But in introducing undulations the builder of courses must consider the shot which is to find the green. What could be more unfair than the introduction of pronounced undulations in a green upon which the player is supposed to pitch? It is obvious that two balls, each receiving the same amount of under-cut, might strike within a foot of each other, one on the ascending slope and the other just beyond, where the ground falls away. Every golfer knows the action of these two balls and appreciates how much the element of luck has figured. Consequently, undulations should be reserved for greens other than those upon which we are to pitch.

The manner in which the guarding pits are built into the sides of the putting greens is most important. Shallow traps are of little value either as hazards or impressive features. Generally, we depend upon the earth from nearby pits for the fill with which our greens are built up, and if the greens are conceived boldly the traps will take care of themselves. In my opinion, there is little excuse for digging pits less than two feet six inches deep and up to five feet. Naturally, the deeper pits must be of greater area.

Sometimes water will not permit the digging of pits to any considerable depth. Then it is necessary to build the pits from the ground up, as it were. But if our hazards are to provide character for the greens, they must be something more than holes in the ground. Their shapes should be irregular, and the mound work, ruggedly natural.

In building greens in flat country, the use of scoops will be found to be very valuable. With them, grass hollows of considerable extent may be formed, pulling the earth to the green site and thus creating a plateau, which will appear even higher than reality because of the break of the hollow in front.

In our limited space it is possible to touch but lightly upon this topic of green character, but the main thought is here: Construct your greens boldly and naturally, remembering at all times from which side of the fairway the approach is to come and the character of the club with which the approach is to be made.

No. 5 Center Course, Ridgewood Country Club: This hole will play in the Ryder Cup matches at about 210 yards.

23 THE CART BEFORE THE HORSE

IT IS NOT DIFFICULT for the golf architect to analyze holes, which he has seen or constructed himself, to set forth his views of their virtues and faults, but to sit down in cold blood and illustrate a hole, the like of which he has never seen anywhere or even heard of, is like biting off a rather big mouthful.

When the thinking readers look at this article's sketch, doubtless many will come to the conclusion that the writer has gone daft. Truth to tell, when the idea first found its way into my skull, I mentally pooh-poohed it away, but it persistently came back home like the cat that one is trying to lose, until finally it stuck, and frankly I am unable to assert whether I am sorry or not. It is not because the hole is different from any which I have seen that causes me to hesitate in presenting it for your consideration (for I glory in seeing any hole which is original yet sound), but rather because, in one vital essential, it flies deliberately into the face of golf conventions. It puts the cart before the horse. Actually it calls for the approach before the long shot, which usually is played from the teeing ground. At first glance it has all the earmarks of a freak, and as such I was inclined to regard it for a while, but after thoughtful consideration there came the conviction that it was not beyond the bounds of reason after all. But it is only a suggestion for debate. I am not prepared to assert that the hole would prove a success nor will I until it has been tried out, but I go on record as stating that it will be tried when natural conditions warrant and an indulgent green committee will grant permission. Let us turn to the sketch.

We find a limited fairway, practically bounded on three sides by water, and on the left by a pronounced slope. A tee shot of two hundred yards must run into difficulties, in this instance water, although any sort of waste land might serve the same purpose as does the lake. Obviously a well-calculated iron shot must hold this strip of fairway before the green can possibly be reached with a long brassey for the second. That is all there is to the hole. A study of the sketch will show, I think, the troubles which must follow an erring tee-shot, and also the easy route to the green for the only moderately proficient player, who is content to get home in three. I conceive this particular hole to measure between 400 and 420 yards, local

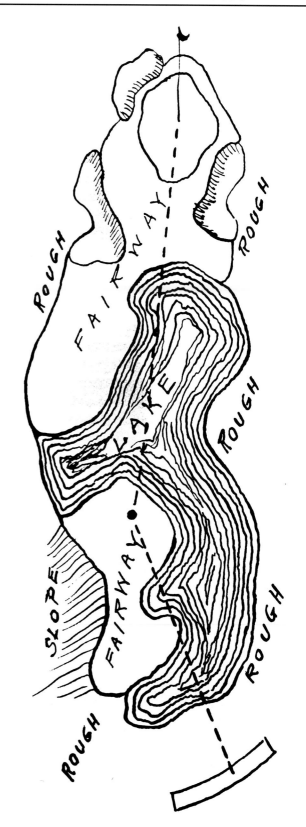

conditions of course determining this. Frankly it is not a type which one would wish to encounter frequently, but let us imagine that such a hole had to be faced occasionally; would it be a freak or objectionable at all?

Simply because it is customary to whale into a drive from a teeing ground, do we find any reason why a player should not be called on to use another club with all the precision of placing his ball in a fairway as he would use in playing a tee-shot to a green? Can we call any hole a bad one, which demands that the player use his head and then play an absolutely sound golf stroke before he may find par figures a possibility? The hole, which is illustrated, in my humble opinion, calls for golf of the highest order and golf which is far from child's play.

There is much more, or there should be much more, to the shots from the teeing ground than always slogging them out to the limit. Certainly we should have holes, and many of them, where the longest of drives gains a distinct advantage, but when all is said and done, the greatest holes are those which place almost as great a premium on direction as length.

Sometimes we encounter holes which have been given over to local rulings and no penalty is exacted when an extra long drive may run into a ditch, road or some other natural hazard, which happens to exist at a spot, unfortunate under some conditions. I think that good golfers do not condone these local rules. If such a hazard exists, no matter whether it punish the super-drive or not, it should be considered and the shot played with fitting judgment.

I doubt very much if I would deliberately manufacture a hole of this description. As a matter of fact there seems to me small excuse for manufacturing any hole when nature may offer anything which, with a little thought and ingenuity, may be turned to our needs. But is likely that in many places there exists some corner, from which a way must be found, and this cart-before-the-horse hole may very well be resorted to rather than blindly following the conventional type, which may prove exceedingly tame and mediocre at this particular spot.

It is certain that many of the most ordinary holes in the country to-day are ordinary because the customary types have been followed too strictly. Why not steadfastly close our mind's eye to every hole which we have ever seen or heard of when we build? It is far better to dig into the ten million golf holes which have never been built than to duplicate some of those which are almost as old as the game itself. Not that some of the ancient holes are not great. They are great where they already exist but how entirely out of place they are when nature does not cooperate. The hat which Madame gives the cook after wearing it for a bit, seldom looks so well on the other's head.

This reference to the attempts to duplicate features, which have appealed to the committeeman on some other course, brings to mind some of the most atrocious examples of putting-green construction imaginable. Often the greens are built well enough and sometimes they follow the contours of the originals faithfully (although not usually), but the one vital thing which has been neglected is the thought of the shot which is to find the green. The original green may be beautifully suited to take a full brassey, but the copy may be at the finish of a mashie hole. So let us strive to be as original as possible. But this is digressing from the idea of the placed tee-shot with clubs under the power of driver or brassey.

It may seem that I am rather blowing hot and then blowing cold on this new fangled hole. In any event I am giving you the thought just as it is. It is certain that such a hole would have to be constructed with great care to avoid the suggestion of freakishness. The plateau fairway would have to be shaped up with nearly as much care as would-be given to the building of a putting green. It must be comparatively limited in area or the value of the placement of the tee-shot is lost entirely. A big fairway would spoil the hole entirely.

The hazard, which has to be carried with the second shot, must be sufficiently wide to prevent missed shots, which have found the rough short of the first fairway, from being jammed out and across to the second fairway in a promising position. Naturally the natural local conditions would fix the placement of pits, but the green must be fairly open to receive that long second shot, home.

As I said almost in the beginning, this hole is open to debate and the comments of the readers of this article will be most welcome. Indeed, I should like to have the criticisms and suggestions of every man who reads these lines.

Contouring the Green

The ninth at Winged Foot Golf Club during the 1929 U.S. Open. The picture shows the fine contouring of the green which is for a fine two shot hole and excellence of bunkering for a hole of this length.

IN LOOKING BACK over more than a quarter century of professional work, planning and building golf courses, it is likely that I appreciate, even to a greater extent than the old time players, the gradual change of many features. Those who have entered the field in recent years have little conception of this at all.

Here is an interesting question. In what particulars do the best courses of today differ widely from those good ones of two or three decades past? And it must be admitted that there were many truly great courses in America at the beginning of this century. Certainly few of them would offer an entirely satisfactory test of play now but they very adequately met all the conditions of the day. But the best courses of the present are better, and in the same breath it may be observed that the bad ones today are no better than the bad ones of yesterday, particularly in view of the fact that now there is no excuse for it. Clubs that are more

powerful perhaps but certainly more easily handled, and balls that yield greater distances generally, have changed the types of holes and rendered obsolete others. Before the introduction of the Haskell patented ball the distance of three hundred to three hundred and twenty-five yards, then regarded as a good drive and mashie length, was frequently presented, but now it is looked upon as "Dodo." The reasons are quite obvious and it is not the purpose of this article to waste space and time in golf-kindergarten. Every good golfer knows a bad hole when he plays it and generally he is sufficiently analytical to tell the reason. But aside from the improved implements of play, what has brought about the gradual change of the character of our courses?

The best turf of 1900 was quite the equal of any today. The best architects of that time gave quite as much study to terrain and the proper reception of shots. The

The approach to the ninth at Brook Hollow from a point at the end of a good drive.

contouring of the best greens was excellent and as good as now; better in many instances for then there was not the tendency to depart too far from nature, an unpleasant habit of some of the younger school. It is true that our Teeing Grounds now are more spacious and better conditioned than of old, and certainly our manufactured hazards represent more thought as to location and natural looking contours. What then is the greatest difference; the most marked improvement of the championship course of 1930 over that of 1900? Undoubtedly the shot to the green.

The relationship between the properly placed shot to the fairway and the following one to the green is the real standard of measuring the merit of any course. The course stands or falls through the character of its one-shot holes. This is true. But these features along will not pull through by its boot-straps the course that does not offer, on all other holes, the clean, accurate shot to the pin after thoughtful, skillful placement of the preceding stroke. In the opinion of the master players of the game this is the true acid test of a championship course.

Not so long ago Tommy Armour declared that putting was given entirely too much prominence in golf, that its value was too great when compared to other shots. I quite agree with him and we are in no hopeless minority by any

means. Some years ago a national champion advocated a half inch enlargement of the cup to more nearly balance the values of golf shots. Others have even suggested the abolition of the cup itself altogether and making the green a sort of target affair. Perish the thought! Tinkering with the traditions of the royal and ancient game could only result disastrously. The remedy is not there.

But, it is reasonable to assume that the nearer ends any shot, that finds the green, fairly close to the cup, the less difficult will it be to hole it? If this is true the value of the shot to the green itself is made greater and the putt of less value. And this is as it should be. Contour the moderately sized green to reward in this fashion the more difficult shot from fairway to pin, and putting will have its value, but a truly balanced value.

Naturally enough this may be carried to a ridiculously unfair extreme. It is not suggested that our greens be of the pocket-handkerchief size. Neither is it inferred that they should throw into the hole from all sides as did the old punch-bowl type which were so very popular in their day, peace be to their ashes!

The character of the proper shot that should find any green must regulate the size of the green and the character of its contours. Under normal conditions a green of ten thousand square feet should be quite large enough to receive the longest of shots and this area may well grade down to as little as six thousand for the very short ones.

Extremely large greens breed slovenly play. When any green ceases to command respect it loses its value as a test of that rarest of all strokes—the shot home. The national championships seem to be awarded to courses that place a premium on this fine play, and golfers generally prefer them. "But," some may argue, "do not some of the most notable courses of Great Britain, courses over which they play their championships, present some abnormally large greens? Certainly they do, and sometimes they are copied over here. But may not this be the very reason why American players have shown a marked superiority during recent years? Many of the amateur and professional players who have represented this country in our contest with British golfers, and who have been making such remarkable showings in their championships, declare that the constant playing of close second shots over the better American courses has developed the margin of superiority. It must also be remarked that undeniably fine British players, coming to America and playing under our best conditions, have so greatly improved their games that they are strokes better now.

This much is evident—the more carefully do the shots home have to be calculated and hit, to that extent does general play improve—and after all that seems to be just about what most golfers pray for.

The green, which is raised in the back to offer some "bite" to the shot that is played firmly up to the pin, is typical of modern construction and is taking the place of the absolutely flat greens of other years. But too little attention is paid to raising one side a trifle higher than the other, which sometimes is very desirable. Of course the character of the shot, that should find and hold the green, determines the proper construction. For example, the true

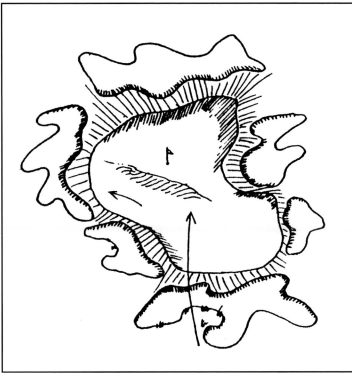

lofted approach, of short or medium length, should work slightly from left to right. Every golfer knows that this underspin causes the ball to check when it strikes ground. Consequently a green, built to receive such a shot should offer every assistance to the ball truly hit with this "work" imparted to it, and a slightly raised right side, or right rear, offers the greatest encouragement to the player. And if the green is to help the correctly played shot, it is but proper that it lend no aid to the ball that comes up with the wrong spin; in fact, such a shot should fall upon a surface which will emphasize its fault.

The sketch represents a green, closely guarded on all sides, designed to take a fairly short lofted approach. It will be noticed that the contour of the right-rear, and even the gradual break, which appears near the center, help to straighten out and hold the slightly sliced shot. The ball, which comes in from right to left, not only receives no help from the green but it is very likely to have its roll hastened to the side pits on the left.

Of course the situation is reversed in the case of a green, constructed to receive a long shot, and such a ball very properly may "show its legs" a bit after it strikes. The flaring up of the left side of such a green will help to straighten out the slightly pulled ball, that is not running too fast. Here, the right side of the green should possess cunning throws to treat the sliced shot with scant ceremony but conduct it directly to retribution.

Another thought which the sketch suggests is the relative values of the front and back pits. I incline to the belief that the rear pits will gather in more balls than those in front, assuming that the approach is in the neighborhood of one hundred yards, but only the careful observation of the play of a hole of this type could determine the point. The shot of this length is one of the most difficult to execute correctly. It is the true wrist-shot with a mashie or similarly lofted iron. It was better played before the advent of the rubber-cored balls of the present day, and the invention of the mashie-niblick. When this length of accurately pitched shot is called for I believe that most of the feebly-hit balls may fall short of the front pits, whose chief value may be estimated

San Francisco's Duel Hole: Looking backward from the green to the teeing ground. Roger Lapham is putting and standing alone, on the right, is Gene Tunney.

by the fear which they inspire, and this causes many strokes to be played much too hard, finding punishment in the rear hazard.

Putting-Greens on modern courses are built entirely to conform with the dictates of the various strokes of golf play, sightliness and harmonious blending with surroundings, and common sense. Without detailed comparison between greens of antiquated and modern type, it will be sufficient to say that the old greens were without character, frequently blind to the approach, located in basins which collected surface water rather than draining it off easily. But by far the worst fault was the flat surface, which offered no encouragement for firm shots played correctly "up to the pin." As course building developed in America, the putting-greens gradually assumed character, opening to approaches after carefully

placed drives. They were raised at the back to give greater "bite" to approaches and to insure good surface drainage. This was a step in the right direction, although often the work was crude and the artificial construction was glaringly apparent. The slopes were severe and unsightly. This, too, was true of artificial hazards and the courses of other days were cluttered with grave-like bunker tops and piles of earth which after a while were referred to as "chocolate drops." But the use of horse scoops in the contouring of greens and hazards enables the builders of modern courses to approach nature very closely in the creation of pleasing undulations which are effective, easily kept in condition and above else harmonious with natural surroundings.

I think that the proper contouring of a course is more readily appreciated by golfers generally than any other department of construction work and the presence of an old-fashioned featureless green would be just as much out of place on an up-to-date course as cobble-stone paving along Fifth Avenue.

Horton Smith playing from one of the traps guarding the ninth hole at Fresh Meadows during the 1930 PGA Championship.

69

25   THE GATEWAY TO THE GREEN

SURELY I feel that I never have attempted a more important contribution to golf course construction than this: the immaculate preparation of approaches to greens. In recent years I have devoted almost the same attention to contouring these as to the putting greens themselves. Obviously this applies to such greens as are reached by long shots from wood or the longer irons and where the bite of the ball is not necessarily "bang-up to the pin." On holes of the long second shot type, it is not sufficient to prepare only the fairway carefully and permit it to end abruptly as it meets the green. True, good greenkeepers always devote extra care to the upkeep of these approaches, and very properly, too, but this is not enough.

I insist that they should be contoured intelligently, with the true shot to the green ever in mind, and prepared and maintained as semi-green.

It does not follow that this construction must be confined to the outstanding courses of rare distinction. A few hours with scoops during the construction days of any course, even the most humble, will serve to fit the approach to the green, give the green a framing which will make it inspiring to see – particularly from a

distance – and generally raise the standard of any course from the so-so type at no great additional cost. But above all, the contouring of the approach adds new zest in playing the shots, particularly in the case of the calculating golfer.

Let us regard some photographs of recent construction work to enable you to visualize the point, as I fear my words lagging behind racing thought may not do. Figure One was photographed from the green, looking back over the line of play, a dog-leg as shown by the dotted line. The shot to the green itself may be anything from a spoon to a long mashie after a well hit drive. Observe how the approach has been contoured so that the slightly shorter driver may have something to play against even though he does not enjoy the same advantage as do the longer hitters. On this particular hole the drive of anything less that 175 yards has little chance of getting home. He most be contented with his 5 by playing discreetly.

Figure Two shows the same approach and green as the shot comes into it. In the illustration, it must be admitted that the flag is placed in a very severe corner, although in reality there is a much greater area to hold

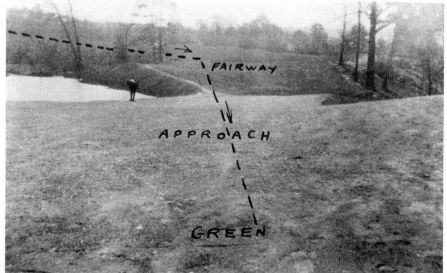

Figure One

Figure Two

a shot than appears in the eye of the camera.

Figure Three shows another green, indicated by the letter "G" and the approach "A." The green has been seeded and the approach has been contoured and spread with manure, preparatory to working it to proper quality for seeding.

Figure Three

It is quite unnecessary to refer to the vexations following good shots to bumpy and unfair approaches. The badly conditioned approach has no place on any course. But the thought of this article is directed to modern methods, ultra-modern if you will, but sensible.

Some of the best holes to be found anywhere show the approaches in a perfectly natural state, with contours in every way admirable. Wherever it is possible, the selection of a natural approach to a green should be considered almost to the extent as that given to the green itself. But nevertheless it is quite possible, at a comparatively little cost, to create contoured approaches which, although artificial, will appear natural.

The approach to the thirteenth hole of the Upper Course at Baltusrol Golf Club.

26

Figure One: This hole from a noted Metropolitan course was reconstructed by reversing the green and tee.

BECAUSE there are infinitely more courses being reconstructed throughout America today than new ones being created, it would seem that the topic of the "madeovers" would be of more general interest than the details of the work of making brand new ones. Probably seventy-five per cent of the demands for my professional services involve reconstruction. Frequently the changes are made after the acquisition of adjoining land for the purpose of adding length to measure up to the distances of the modern "rabbit" ball and generally improved play, but more often the desire to change the course is the direct result of a realization that the existing lay-out is faulty, passé, uninteresting or downright bad.

It is not hard to understand that some old courses, designed and constructed twenty to thirty years ago, need considerable revamping to retain prestige. But as a matter of fact, the great majority of the once-noted veteran courses have gone through reconstruction ere now, or they have disappeared from the earth. I refer to American courses, built when this country's grasp of the game was weak and conception exceedingly crude. The many glaring faults of early American course building are well known to seasoned players, and as much has been written about them they have no place in this article. But rather let us regard the causes for changing holes of comparatively recent creation, some of them scarcely dry of the factory paint, so to speak. There comes to mind the real tragedy of one club which has spent nearly nine hundred thousand dollars to acquire its property, club house and course. Within six months they were awake to the bitter realization that the course was an utter failure, yet they resolutely put hand to the plow and began an immediate reconstruction, fortunately to good purpose. The cause of this failure was due entirely to an utter misconception of the true way to lay out the holes. The changes made necessary a most drastic rearrangement from start to finish. Cases such as this fortunately are most unusual, for often enough a drab trend of holes may be rescued by slight deviations from original plans and ingenious reconstruction aided by impressive contouring and landscaping.

I recall only one course which seemed quite unworthy of improvement. The original selection of property was so unfortunate and the construction so mangled that it seemed fit only to be scrapped. Eventually the acquiring of adjoining property, which at the time was unobtainable, saved the course.

As I regard the many sick courses I have had to doctor, the maladies appear to be about as follows:

Unintelligent planning and construction. Either of the above without the other. Tearing away to various degrees from sound plans and directions by green committees or their successors.

Hasty selections of property without proper analysis of terrain, soil conditions or drainage.

Purchasing property for a golf course principally because there happens to be a fine collection of buildings, seemingly suitable for club house purposes. The chances are that the main building may cause a deformed course to be built to fit the site, and after great expense the old house fails to provide the real conveniences of a new, carefully planned plant.

A collection of contoured greens which have no real reason for being formed other than they look like something someone has seen on another course. This applies to all glaringly artificial atrocities.

Ignoring obviously fine natural conditions for the above abortive efforts. Raising pulpit-like teeing grounds when there is no occasion. Elevating greens and hazards with steep, formal slopes, which not only are offensive to the eye but a tribulation to the greenkeeper. Blind holes— particularly greens which should be gained by pitched shots.

Too many sand pits—and I mean this most emphatically. Too many American courses are made hideous and uninviting by an unnecessary number of sand pits, particularly those which bother only the very poor player. If the holes are of proper lengths and *each green contoured and guarded intelligently* the poor shots will not ride a man home. For example, the duffer who can only slice a drive a hundred and fifty yards, does not have to find himself buried in a sand pit to take iron into his soul. Let us pay more attention to the par figure player who only too often scurries around without courting much disaster, because the hazards have been placed only to add to the tribulations of the hosts who feel a good shot only now

Spring Lake Golf and Country Club: The old course at Spring Lake, remodeled along modern lines is one of the best along the Jersey coast. Located conveniently near the Atlantic Ocean are both the Monmouth and the Essex and Sussex hotels.

and then. Not that our courses should be entirely open. Far from that! But golf should permit finessé; carries should be graded and elective—not obligatory. I firmly believe that over-bunkering American courses may do more to dampen enthusiasm by making play too irksome than any modern ball of long flight may ever work evil by making play too easy. May I repeat before continuing with our list of disease? One of the worst of all the ills is "Bunkeritis," the mad desire of some green committees to have men groping around eighteen holes in sand, straining their glazed and agonized eyes for a bit of fairway.

Now to continue:

1. Greens that don't drain.
2. Greens that drain too much.
3. Greens too large for small shots.
4. Greens too small for long shots.
5. Greens too freakish for any shot. (I once heard a certain hole lauded because in an Open tournament the pros averaged nearly six for the hole. This alone proved that the hole was not good—a freak pure and simple.)
6. Changing a hole because a certain class player did not like it. (This rather suggests the time-worn alibi and the tendency to praise or condemn wholly because of the good or bad fortune of the individual.)
7. Holes playing directly into hill slopes.
8. Holes playing along slopes rather than into them.
9. Climbs to higher levels too suddenly and not gradually enough to make play not arduous
10. Holes laid out backwards.

This may read so strangely that our partial list of evils may as well terminate here to allow consideration of this remark. In the old days particularly, and now-a-days, too, if there happened to exist some very outstanding feature such as a lake or quarry hole, the builder of courses would naturally hop to it with alacrity, and only too often would this hole begin then and there. The teeing ground would be built hard by on the very edge or brink and casting out most anywhere ahead the line of play would be directed to

a green, frequently located in an unattractive, featureless area. It would seem quite enough to throw fear into a man's heart as he stood on that tee and gazed down into the fearsome maw, which waited for his *topped* drive. Here again we encounter the old tendency to punish fearfully the very bad shot. Such a hole may be considered to be laid out backwards. The green and its approaches may be regarded as the most vital part of any hole. No hole is any greater than its green— its finish. Invariably the outstanding natural hazard will make a fine hole if it is near the green and not the teeing ground. A photograph is offered to illustrate the point. On a certain well-known Metropolitan course there once was the hole of the photograph with a teeing ground on the brink of the huge excavation now shown in sand. There was nothing to the drive, other than duffer fear, and absolutely no featuring second shot to the flat meadow green. When the course was reconstructed three holes were reversed, each to its betterment and particularly this one. The photograph shows players making their way to the green after their second shots. Of course, the green needed some little making on the site of the former teeing ground, but the present tee shot is from the old green—and that is about all it was good for. The cost of reconstructing the hole was slight.

A rough sketch of a lake possibly may further illustrate the point. Here is a body of water, and water hazards are unquestionably very popular if introduced in moderation. Naturally the possibilities here are numerous. No. 1 shows the old-fashioned method—a shot to a plain green from the very edge of the water. Almost any thing other than an absolute top would clear the hazard. A fine player would fear nothing—but the duffer might have his troubles through fear alone. Such a hole is featureless so far as play is concerned, although picturesque. But the lake may add its beauty to other arrangements which certainly will be more like golf. For example, the arrangement of No. 2 is better, but No. 3 seems to be still better, for here the carry of the water is quite elective. The player may get closer to the pin by playing a more accurate carry of the pond. It seems that these three arrangements are quite obvious.

27

SINCE the end of the war there has been an unprecedented activity in course construction and reconstruction. Everywhere green committees are planning improvements. In many instances the committees realize the short-comings of their courses by reason of their own play, in other cases possibly some well-known golfer, whose opinion should bear weight, has criticized bluntly or given candid reply when pressed. But frequently the good work is started because there exists the conviction that a hole or two certainly needs radical changing, and beyond this only a vague idea that the remainder may not be worthy in the eyes of the discriminating golfers. Generally there is to be found the very laudable desire to remedy ills, but not always is the real complaint altogether apparent to those who would help it.

Perhaps a short analysis of the most common faults will be welcomed—in brief, the sure symptoms of ailing holes.

The invalid most often come across is the pasty faced hole which is quite featureless and the world of golf is filled with them. I refer to the broad fairway, stretching away to an immense green which may be reached with a very ordinary second shot from either side of the fairway, a hole which is forgotten as soon as played because it never caused one to think of any relation between the shots. Most holes of this low order may be helped without serious inconvenience or expense. However, if the green slopes away from the shot (higher in the front than in the rear) the cure will be more costly.

Another invalid is the distance which is just beyond the reach of any normal drive and yet perfectly open to any two shots, one of which has been atrociously hit. This is a common fault, too.

There is the old-fashioned type with the green perched on the very pinnacle of a hill, a variety which usually develops freak and trick approaches. Walking straight up a hill-side is really as uninteresting as playing the shot. Side-hills are not desirable but they are not past curing.

Then there is the funnel-like green with every remote slope doing its utmost to throw all shots to the flag. Usually such holes are badly drained.

A pretty stretch of meadow land, with its winding stream, may exert a strong appeal, but often in the spring that same picturesque brook may be an angry torrent, eating its way wherever it may or flooding acres of fairway and green. This is a more complicated case but not hopeless.

Whenever you come across monotonously long holes, obviously introduced to bolster up the length of a course, dwarfed by too many short ones, be sure you see a patient for no far future day.

Turf, which generally is soft and ready to swallow the ball, cannot be accepted in these days. It insures disagreeable golf and unfair golf, too. This is not only true of the fairway but of an habitually soggy putting green. Equally bad is the flint-like sections, from which the ball bounds and rushes on like some mad thing. Sick holes!

There are many more varieties but it seems no harm to mention these few, for they are common. When you play a pitched shot to a blind green without the satisfaction of observing the actual pitch and run, or pitch and stop, do you find any zest in the shot? Few do, and for this reason the blind green is seen far less often than of yore.

So it is with bad, sick holes generally. If they afford you but scant pleasure, make up your mind that they are not good. If any hole permits you to play it in a lethargic, unthinking manner, that hole is thoroughly sick. I do not mean to infer that a hole to be good must rack a man's soul. Far from it. Golf ceases to be a recreation for many thousands when it makes a man sweat blood, although all right enough on courses laid out with the only thought of providing a stern test for the cracks. But let your golf courses make you think a little, and then you will glory in the knowledge of having accomplished something. It is a thrill which the sick hole cannot give. It's no fun to kick the stuffing out of a corpse!

FOR MANY YEARS the Putting Green was regarded by the average golfer as an especially well turfed spot on each hole, where the Putter was used to finish off the play of that particular hole, by stroking the ball into the cup. Many even contended that the comparatively short strokes of the Putter quite overbalanced the values of strokes generally. A close analysis probably would prove this contention.

But in these modern times we have come to regard the putting greens as something far different than just nice velvety stretches for a "sissy" finish after several strenuous and skillful strokes that ate up distances. If you will contemplate a green as something that fits more definitely into the scheme of play than in the old days, where the play TO the cup from a distance is really a part of the subsequent play ON the green itself, I think that the contours and bunkering of the flag areas will present a new significance. When you once have the picture of this point, let your mind roam again from the conventional thoughts, and focus on this idea—Golf is, after all, a game of attack and defense —your own attack on every hole with the ingenious

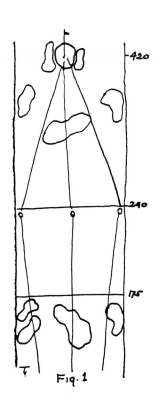

Fig. 1

design of the green itself, an inanimate defense there ever to thwart you provided you have not maneuvered thoughtfully and skillfully to get into a proper position to attack.

When we find this we know that the course itself is a great one. It is this thought that is a part of the P.G.A. doctrine, which has been assigned me to preach and to make my point as understandable as possible, I have prepared two rough sketches. Shall we study them briefly?

Figure One represents a thoroughly conventional hole of two-shot length over a fairway, which is fifty yards wide up to the green, 420 yards away. The green itself is typical of those to be found from one end of our land to the other. It faces directly down the fairway with side pits. As a matter of strategic defense these mechanically precise affairs cannot truly be said to *guard* the green. They gather in loose balls.

At a distance of 240 yards out we represent three long drives. Now as a matter of fact the placement of these drives matters but little for the green offers an equally attractive reception to the second shot from the left, center or right. The zone across the fairway out to 175 yards is literally infested with traps (sometimes the mid-trap is missing). They are so close to the teeing ground that even a half-hit shot of the par-player rarely encounters any of them. In brief they trap only the very best efforts of that great 90% of our golfers, who are striving to break 90. To the "hundred-gaffers" they are headaches. To the greenkeeper they are nuisances and to the club budget they are serious drains. Frequently there are more of these in the zone of

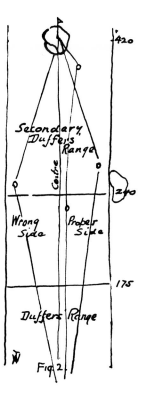

Fig. 2

the approach, but observe again—not once does one make the hole a bit stiffer save in the case of the duffer. Eight or nine of these useless pits might well be eliminated, with but two traps possibly taking their places, as I endeavor to show with Figure Two.

Here the most obvious difference is the change of the long axis of the green, with the introduction of one pit close-up on *one* side (on the left in this instance). This I call the Master Pit. It would be placed on the right provided the long axis of the green had been contoured to favor the approach from the left side of the course, rather than the right as in the sketch. This arrangement definitely divides the fairway into halves. It is evident that any drive in the left half is on the WRONG side. A player does not find it necessary to drive into any pit on that side to convince him that he is wrong. The Master Pit problem rather well convinces him of that.

It is quite evident that the very Defense of the green makes it necessary to Place the tee-shot within 25 yards of the center of the fairway rather than within double that range as in Figure One. And keeping in mind the fact that we want to make the par-players meet even greater tests than usual, we probably would place a driving pit far out, on the very side of the fairway where the proper placement is to be made. In addition to the probable route of the golfer, who walks with par, I have shown that of the fairly proficient golfer who cannot pass 200 yards. He cannot hope to reach home in this instance but he may place his

second in a correct position for his attack of the green with his third, having exactly the same chance to secure his par as has the more expert player has to snare his bird from the longer range of his second.

It will be noticed that all other pits, which are shown on Figure One, are removed entirely from the scheme of Figure Two and these areas designated as Duffers' Ranges. No one really cares a lot what the poor old duffer does anyhow? He is not a serious factor in golf. But he is a mighty important one. He wants his pleasure and we contend that he should have all that possibly may be brought to him as he golfs as best he can. These superfluous pits are not only unpleasant but they are very expensive to maintain. Why should the golf courses of America have so much money wasted on their construction and maintenance for no other purpose than to drive away from the clubs and the game the very men, who are so vitally necessary to the existence of the game.

The fifteenth green on the San Antonio municipal course. It is a two-shotter requiring a well placed mashie second. The line of play is from the bottom center of the photograph.

THE SKETCH, which accompanied our last article, in order to illustrate and entire fairway had to be so small that only the position of the Master Trap, guarding the green, was generally indicated. There was nothing about it to suggest any contour or sand arrangement. As the manner of showing sand must be regarded as something of considerable importance, I believe it is timely to draw particular attention to it by means of the more comprehensive drawing on this page and also by comment.

My sketch shows sand tucked about a green in such a manner as to open the green to a second shot, that has been accurately placed on the proper side of the fairway. It may be recalled that my last article definitely declared that greater interest was being introduced to our modern golf by a simplified method of trapping, which rewarded placements of the tee-shots, on one side of the fairway or the other. Of course it must not be misconstrued to infer that I contend that this system should be invariable. But often enough it will bring with it pleasing variety with better play. In this instance the functioning of the Master Pit is very apparent, I think, but here two pits are used to

close the green from the Wrong Side while one more appears on the opposite side, whereas our former sketch showed none at all there. This is optional of course for variety's sake.

However the real topic of my paper concerns the arrangement of the sand in pits, guarding greens. In my travels about the country I observe numerous fancies in this respect. In some instances the sand is confined entirely to the floors of the pits (often enough huge areas) with absolutely no sight of the sand from any distance and frequently only when one looks directly down into the cavern from close range. Generally this is not favorably regarded but still it exists for no better reason than that it has done so for years on that particular course. In the past few seasons of golf, various patterns of sand-irons have been designed and are in general use. The crude old niblick no longer thumps balls out from the maws of sand hazards. So cleverly have these heads been patterned that it is no longer much of a trick to pitch a bunkered ball up against the pin. As a consequence guarding pits have lost their effectiveness to an amazing extent. Really sand is more ornamental than useful now-a-days and some have made so bold as to express opinion that it eventually may disappear from our courses all together. This is a rather far cry but it is certain that there is less of it used every year.

Now I have referred to the sand that is hidden away from sight. There is still another treatment with white showing up to the very brinks of the traps. Often the turf, where it meets the sand, is frilled into fantastic lines, "frivolously ginger-bready" if I may use the expression. But certainly it is far from natural-looking and while better than the first method, it utterly fails (as I see it) to convey the picture of sand, wind-blown up into rugged slopes, or nestling naturally into slopes. This latter effect is what I refer to when I speak of "Tucked in traps." I have endeavored in my sketch to convey this last idea.

This effect cannot be obtained simply by digging holes in the ground. When this alone is done you have your sand hidden in a big cheese. To show it off the depth of the trap depends upon the heighth of side of the green as it

blends to meet the trap, which tucks in to the slope. Have I succeeded in making this point clear? The depth and character of the sand-trap, three feet deep, may depend on the distance that the hole has been dug down (which is wrong) or by the three feet that it blends up to meet its surroundings (which is right).

One more detail which is often overlooked. If clean white sand is not procurable—better none at all or a grassed-hollow. (It is just about as hard to pitch a ball accurately from a grassy depression these days as it is to knock it up cold from a sand pit with one of trick clubs.) Dirty sand is not good to contemplate nor pleasant to knock about in. The content of clay packs down and then what have you? Under such a condition the hazard loses all virtue. Certainly a splash of white sand here and there does go a long way to dress up a golf course. But don't buy it by the car loads; use it with discrimination and above all—put it where it may be seen.

"Little Tilly," the short 13th hole on the course of the San Francisco Golf and Country Club.

The fourteenth green at San Francisco Golf and Country Club.

30 SLOPES? BLEND THEM!

THE STEEP SLOPING of banked earth is one of the chief abominations of American courses as I have encountered them during a complete girdling of the United States during the past seven months. As is generally known, I am the course consultant of the P.G.A. and in that capacity I have to examine courses critically, point out their weaknesses, put my finger on unnecessary and expensive details and suggest corrections. While these objectionable features vary considerably there is one, sticking up like a sore toe, which I am rather sure to find on ninety per cent of the courses throughout the country today—steep slopes.

These are not only unsightly because of the unnaturalness of appearance, but costly to maintain. In these modern times with up-to-date equipment to aid in the speed and economy of upkeep, hand labor should be reduced to a minimum. Consequently the contouring of our courses should be accomplished in such a manner as to permit of as much cutting with power-mowers as may be possible. Experience has taught me that slopes, graded to a ratio of one to six (six feet drawn out to every foot of elevation) may be cut easily by a man seated on a tractor and these gently blended slopes are distinctly a departure from the harsh lines of artificial construction. Keep in mind that one word "Blend." I cannot emphasize it too strongly—Blend your slopes so gently and harmoniously that they cease to be slopes.

Of necessity these contributions cannot be anything but suggestive. If there be worth-while thoughts in them that may develop a greater line of thought in your own minds our object will be gained. Consider then the idea of the blending of all your slopes and the benefits will be more apparent as the idea develops.

This brings me to a variation of the sharp slope evil. In a certain section of the country, where the terrain is so flat and featureless that the necessity of breaking it up constructively is obvious, there exists a common practice, horribly expensive and altogether inadequate. Almost invariably, after the site of a green has been selected, the construction is started at the very back of the green. I insert two rough sectional sketches to illustrate the point. In Figure One, the work of construction was started at point B (the back of the green) and an excavation of possibly four feet has been made to provide fill, with which to raise the green. Often a steam-shovel is used. After the fill has been deposited for the green, the rear of

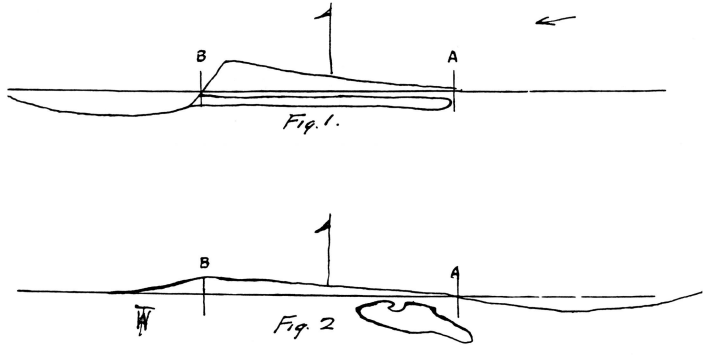

the green often is seven or eight feet higher than the deepest part of the flanking hole in the ground, which usually remains as a hazard after being floored with sand. The presence of flanking pits, directly back of the shot, except in a few instances, cannot be condoned, but more of this later in another article.

Now it will be observed that in Figure 1 there is produced nothing more than a violently raised green with very sharp and steep slopes, grading to the front, Point A, and there is absolutely nothing out in front of the green other than the original flat ground. Approaching players see nothing other than the railroad-like embankment. They do not see the expanse of expensive sand in the rear nor that which extends on the floors on each side with mathematical precision. Yet all this has cost a great deal of money to produce, a great deal more money to maintain, and after all nothing has really been accomplished.

Figure Two shows an entirely different method. In the first place work has been started at Point A, the FRONT of the green. Instead of resorting to the use of a steam shovel, tractor-drawn scoops have contoured the approach to the green, probably never going down deeper than two feet. Even this would automatically raise the original site of the green two feet before any of the fill is deposited. It will not require much imagination to picture exactly what might be done to the approach by introducing suitable contours over a stretch of a hundred feet or more; how much variety might be supplied to the value of shot that is to reach home.

By concentrating at the front and with less than half the work, the view of the hole is very different in the eyes of approaching players. Comparatively little sand, drawn up properly into the front slopes of the green, will be far more impressive and valuable as hazards, particularly if distributed according to the Master Pit idea. It is obvious that with the excavated earth, scooped out from the approach, the green itself may be attractively contoured with all slopes naturally blended. All of this blending of contours can be done so easily that the cutting of everything with a tractor mower would be a matter of course.

Possibly the best thought of this paper may be found in this idea of emphasizing the approach to the greens and the fronts of the greens themselves. The breaks of the ground in front of the greens are of the utmost importance and so frequently neglected as to make us wonder. Really I regard the idea of contouring approaches as one of the best of any employed in modern golf course construction.

The approach to the eighteenth green at Fresh Meadow Country Club, Flushing, L.I., host of the USGA Open Championship.

31   SOLID MOUND WORK

IT HAS BEEN SAID that the reputation of a course depends upon the character of its one-shot holes, and while there is much wisdom in this observation, there are other features which either make or break a course. No matter how excellent the distances may be or how fortunate the location of the putting greens, or how cunning the placement of the hazards, if great care is not taken in the building, the course never will be notable. For instance, a putting green which may be most impressive in some country, might be duplicated in another section where it would be without distinction and out of place. This also applies to hazards, and it is of these that I will devote a bit of space.

Let us assume that we have found a most excellent spot for a hazard. Without a doubt any one of several types would exact its just penalty, but there must be one distinct type best suited to this particular place. We must not permit the lines of our hazards to clash with the surrounding country.

They may remind us of the houses of the *nouveau riche* in which are to be found in the same rooms a riot of decorations, a lurid Navajo rug quarreling with the portieres, or a Japanese screen distinctly unfriendly with the Chippendale chair.

An up-to-date variation of solid mound work: Here the rough sides have been turfed, but the sand has been introduced to relieve the monotony and tufted grass planted in an attempt to imitate dune growth. Lyme grass is admirable for this

So it is on our courses. A rugged, dune-like creation which well might find a place on a seaside course, would be quite out of harmony with gently undulating meadow land. To be sure, the formation in each instance might be similar, but the lines should be different. Each particular locality supplies its own models for mound work, and in designing them the architect ever must keep the surroundings in mind.

Tracts broken up by grassy hollows and mounds are effective and picturesque on inland courses, but along a bleak coast the same formation might be utterly undesirable; in any event, the design would have to be conceived in a more rugged fashion. Often upon some courses we find it desirable to change completely our types where immediate surroundings vary. For instance, one fairway, extending along a valley meadow, might find a hazard area coming to meet it in friendly undulations, but perhaps a few hundred yards distant a gaping quarry hole would have as its neighbors pits of equally severe aspect.

Of course, nothing could be more grotesque than the precise kop-bunkers of other days. Then, no matter where the course happened to be, these coffin-like formations were placed with precision. After a while attempts to imitate Nature were observed more frequently, but even now this inclination is far too infrequent.

In 1911 I planned the course at Shawnee. On the hole which is illustrated in this article, a considerable area was broken up by grass mounds and hollows. Every effort was made to have them appear like a natural formation, and when they had been thrown up, the workmen were made to walk all over them in order to obliterate any regular lines. This huge grass hazard has proved to be very effective, and I can recommend a similar treatment in any section where it is found desirable to have forbidden ground of considerable extent.

Such mound work is not costly to produce. It is simply a matter of staking out the base lines of the mounds; figuring the proper distances between the bottoms of the finished mounds, and then digging from one to the other, throwing up the earth between the stakes. At first there undoubtedly will be a tendency to get these staked sections too close, and when the various slopes meet, there may be not sufficient room to permit the player to swing his club properly. Of course, the floor between the mound bases should be broken up, too, for it is not intended that the player should be able to play out without difficulty, but at the same time he should be given every opportunity for getting his club back without hindrance.

The question of surface drainage must be considered, and the whole floor of a similar area must be modeled in such a way as to include the natural drainage from one end to the other, and although immediately after the first rough work is completed, and before seeding, there may appear to be moist spots after a rain, these should cause no apprehension, for the water will be carried away more readily when all is covered by grass.

The usual attempt at mound work usually results in horribly symmetrical "chocolate drops," with an arrangement which suggests the display in a confectioner's shop window. Yet it requires no more work and no more expense to build along natural and effective lines. There is a great deal of horse sense in golf architecture, after all, and imagination, too.

The Shawnee Course was laid out by the writer some five years ago. In the hole

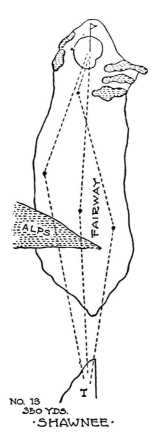

NO. 13
350 YDS.
·SHAWNEE·

represented, the area marked, "Alps" is broken up by rugged mound work, and presents a very stiff carry from the teeing-ground. It will be observed that one route to the hole finds nothing to be carried at all, but in taking this road the conservative player requires three strokes before the green is reached in safety.

A unique feature is the diagonal teeing-ground, one hundred feet in length, which not only permits of lengthening the carry, but also makes it possible to change the angle entirely.

From the sketch it may seem that a long second from the fairway opposite the Alpinization should find no great difficulty in holding the green after successfully clearing the guarding pits, but it must be remembered that the slope to the flag from this angle makes the effort dangerous. The approach should come "straight-on" or, better still, slightly from the left. If a long, wild drive clears the mound district, which is very unlikely, the rough on that side is troublesome.

Natural mounds on the sixth hole at Somerset Hills.

THE GOLF ARCHITECT devotes about three quarters of his time to the planning of improvements and extending old courses. Green Committees in all parts of the country are keenly alive to the realization that holes of faulty design and construction, monotonous holes and those which expose players to danger, must be eliminated. A featureless and poor hole has no place on a modern course. To be sure there is always an element in every club which is opposed to changes, but nowadays those who attempt to deter the work of modernizing courses are of the great minority.

However, it is very proper that the rank and file of golfers should be given some idea of the demands which the new holes will make of his limited skill. The player of very ordinary ability naturally fears that a stiffened course may present fearsome features to rob his rounds of pleasure. As a matter of fact the golf architect of today is a good friend of the duffer. Let us consider a first class two-shot hole for example, a hole which is calculated to call for a full brassey after a well-hit drive. The actual yardage of a hole of this type will vary with conditions, some turf yielding far greater distance than others. But let us assume that the hole in question is located on an inland course of average speed, and that under normal weather conditions the best players are compelled to use wood for both shots to cover the four hundred and sixty yards between teeing-ground and green. The length of this hole alone will place the green beyond the range of the duffer's two healthiest swipes, and if the fairway were absolutely barren of hazards, the "three-figure" man will require three strokes and possibly more. His poorly played shots are vexations enough without digging pit-falls to add to his sorrows. Yet on hundreds of courses we find old-fashioned bunkers, marring the scenery at a point about one hundred and forty yards from the teeing ground, hazards which extend squarely across the line of play and which call for a drive to carry the trouble from crack and duffer alike.

Now it is safe to assert that in the average golf club there are fully twenty-five per cent of the players who cannot average one hundred and forty yards in carry, and a goodly number who cannot make the distance at all even with the long-flying balls of the present day. With such a hazard, many a player must of necessity drive off in desperate effort, feeling in his heart that certain disaster awaits him, yet hoping that some lucky chance may yield a fair shot for his second.

The experts certainly will give the hazard no thought. They can half-hit their drives and still carry well over. In brief, the hazards of yesterday trap only bad shots, while those of the present gather in the "nearly good" ones of the fellows who formerly hooked and sliced their long ones without punishment. We are building hazards, or designing our holes to include natural ones, in such a manner as to grade the carries, with suitable rewards for each successful effort. The scratch player is forced to hit his longest and best to negotiate the carry which will open up the green to the best advantage for his second. Often enough he is called on for a carry of one hundred and eighty yards or more, fully forty or fifty yards longer than before; while the medium and poor players have to contend with a greatly shortened carry and likely none at all.

While, as I have said, the courses generally are structurally and strategically improved over those of a few years back, yet there are enough of the Cheap-John, amateurish sort, rather cluttered with sand pits that cost money to maintain for no other purpose than to discourage the very players at golf, who need encouraging most. When speaking of these abominations in my reports to the P.G.A. for brevity's sake I simply call them D.H.'s (short for Duffer's Headaches). I am thoroughly delighted by the reaction of green committees everywhere to our doctrine of the elimination of these relics of golf's dark age.

33 INTRODUCING SAND INTO THE BUNKER

I HAVE LONG OBSERVED that surprisingly few courses show evidence of proper introduction of sand into bunker slopes and floors. In the building of sand pits at greens and through the fairway, the work usually calls for the use of scoops, removing earth and fill generally from one area and depositing it over another area, close by, and thus providing material for building up impressively and contouring along natural lines. This removal of fill leaves excavations of generous proportions, particularly if the building-up has been done vigorously and impressively, as it should be. As the sloping banks are grassed they meet the floor of the excavated area and if nothing further was done about it there would be this condition—monotonous banks of grass meeting the flat floor, which frequently is covered with sand.

Now the covering of these tremendous floors requires a great deal of sand, an alarmingly expensive item when the work is remote from sections where clean, white sand is to be had. The proper treatment of the excavated areas requires a far less amount of sand and at the same time produces a blending of sand and grass in harmonious framing of the green itself and bringing into full view of the player much of the sand of the hazard which otherwise is not visible from any distance when it is confined to a flat floor. Obviously this makes necessary the introduction of sand into the slopes and a great reduction of the floor area of the excavation, which now in reality becomes a guarding pit. This reduction is accomplished by contouring the floor of the pit, bringing long and gradual slopes into it from the fairway sides and grassing these, thus reducing by a half or more frequently three-quarters the floor of the pit and the necessary quantity of sand, which now is confined to a much smaller area closer to the outside slopes of the green and eating well up into these slopes, from which the turf has been removed to receive it. It is quite obvious that a little ingenuity in working the sand into the grassed slopes will produce an entirely natural appearance of wind-blown sand in great variety.

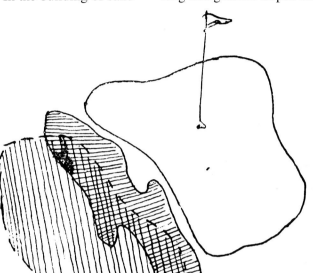

Figure One

Unfortunately, many attempts to cut the sand into slopes is done in a mechanical and formal manner, without producing a pleasing effect or one that is free of artificial—in brief, entirely natural. The sanded slopes, if done properly, will put a stop to the use of putters in getting out of guarding pits. No one really wants to do this, but most anyone will do it when good results are to be had with little effort. Of course, the old-fashioned steep wall, bricked with sod, will stop the practice without any question, but the sanded bank will do it, too.

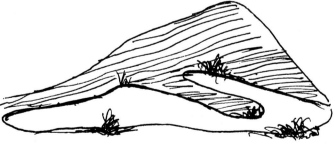

Figure Two

The sketches are from a page of my note book, and drawn crudely to answer the question of the green committee chairman, who showed a green as outlined with a huge pit on the left, as indicated by the dotted lines.

There was nothing else other than the sloping banks of the green. The irregularly shaped area, indicated by the horizontal lines, shows the new lines of sand eating into the slopes of the green and extending down into the present pit. The remainder of this pit will now be contoured and grassed. Any hazard that is worthy of the name will not offer a large, flat floor, and this is particularly true through the fairway, where it is small punishment for the erring player. Great hazard areas had better be a combination of undulating, tough-grassy stretches and sand. Let it exact a true penalty but not one that is unnecessarily severe. This applies more particularly to inland courses than to those not far from the sea, where natural stretches of sandy hazard are encountered so frequently: the great majority of American courses are inland, and hazard areas have to be made. Figure Two is another rough sketch from my note book used in answering the questions of the same green committeeman. It was intended to illustrate the easy slopes of fairway mounds with the sand eating into them in a natural and somewhat rugged fashion. Break up the fairway hazards sufficiently and it will stop to a great extent the getting of distance from them.

One of the best in the world—number 10 at Winged Foot.

The Newport Country Club, one of the original five clubs to form the United States Golf Association. This picture, taken during the final of their Annual Invitation Tournament, shows the thirteenth putting green.

34 THE REAR GUARD GREEN

THIS SKETCH illustrates a satisfactory method of grading punishment to fit the crime in the rear of a green designed to receive a full pitch. Whenever a full pitch from mashie or medium iron is demanded, a premium should be paid for the regulated strength as well as the direction of the shot, and consequently such greens very properly are guarded in the rear.

To make the penalty proportionate to the error, the green may be built as shown in the sketch.

Here three distinct areas are indicated: A, the green proper; B, a grassed hollow falling away in the rear to a sand pit, C. The green itself raising in the back will hold an accurate pitch without permitting the proper shot to trickle into the grassed hollow, which however offers a medium penalty to the ball which is a trifle over strong. It is obvious that the more drastic punishment is found for the much over played shot into C.

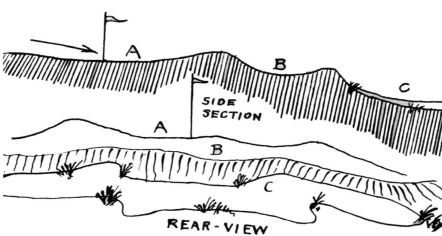

Number 12 green, par 4 at Golden Valley C.C., Minnesota. Notice the contour from back to front—unforgiving if long.

35 TEEING GROUNDS

YEARS AGO TEEING grounds almost invariably were small and mathematically formal but early in my career I ruthlessly tore away from these and wherever possible graded large teeing ground areas which permitted of a constant change of the tee plates to suit weather conditions and to lend variety by playing from different angles. The short fourth, the water hole at Baltusrol, with its irregularly shaped teeing ground, somewhat after the fashion of an immense horseshoe, is a sample of this.

It is difficult to understand why so much so-called modern golf construction adheres to antiquated patterns. The chief offense is in the building of teeing grounds. To many it seems apparently that the teeing ground must be built up and terraced. Of course there are slopes which make a terrace necessary, but there are comparatively few instances where the slopes of the terrace may not be made so gentle as to allow cutting with the regular fairway mowers. There should be as little hand-cutting as possible. The ideal teeing ground is nothing more than a great level area, which will permit the placing of the tee-markers in many, many places. These are natural in appearance and not easily worn out if the markers are shifted each day as they should be. Yet it is no unusual thing to see a pawky little platform raising its little, scarred and bald head above a perfectly natural teeing ground, which has been ignored completely. It has cost money to build the offensive, box-like thing and it costs more to keep it cut. Often enough we find courses which are unkempt and poor, not because

The fourth hole at Baltusrol during the 1926 Amateur.

the budget is insufficient but because it is misused.

Maybe I already have had too much to say about teeing grounds, but there is one point which occurs to me and I think that I never have mentioned it. Often when there are two or three teeing grounds provided for one hole, they are laid out in a dead straight line. This not only looks artificial but the arrangement robs the hole of variety. Playing to the fairway from different angles not only is pleasing, but often the wind dictates a different angle almost as much as length.

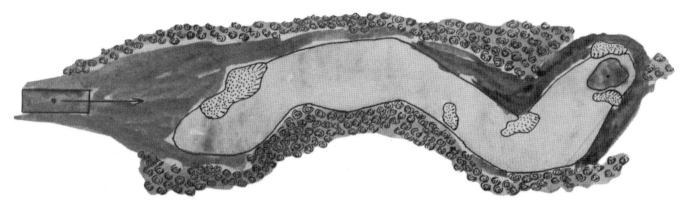

Figure One: An interesting variation of the Author's original double dog's leg.

I WILL ILLUSTRATE briefly several of the unusual holes now under construction at Poxono, in the Valley of the upper Delaware.

It is possible that I have given by imagination a trifle more freedom than usual in designing this course, for it is the first opportunity that I have had in twenty years to build entirely for myself and some of my friends. However, none of the holes are freakish but represent only

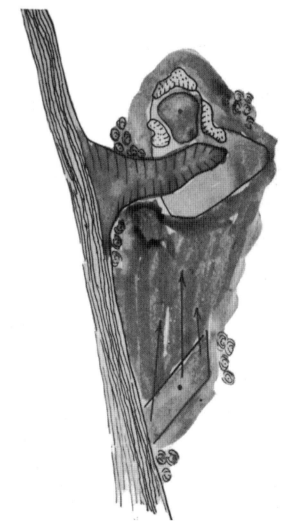

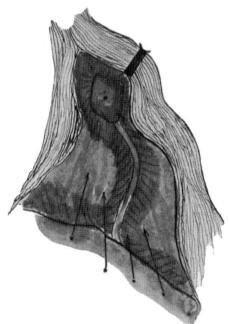

Figure Two: The green is near the intersection of the Delaware and Binniekill. A mashie shot from a wide teeing ground.

Figure Three: The second hole at Poxono. Built on the banks of the Delaware—a jigger or half-iron shot.

sound, enjoyable golf as it appeals to me.

Probably fifteen years ago, I originated the double dog-leg for a plan of a three-shot hole and on many courses, on which I have introduced it, the holes have proved particularly satisfactory, for the length requiring three shots to reach the green is likely to be monotonous unless specially featured. The original double dog-leg provided for the drive and the brassey second to clear intrusions into the fairway, each from the left. Now at Poxono there was a very pleasing terrain which suggested the hole as illustrated by Figure One, and I think the rough sketch will show a rather interesting variation of my original conception.

Figures Two and Three illustrate comparatively short one-shotters, each with an immense teeing ground area which will regulate as desired the distance and angle of play. Figure Three shows the second hole at Poxono, which is built directly along the banks of the Delaware River—a hole of jigger or half-iron length. The placement of the green was suggested by a very pronounced slash (in which, by the way, were found a number of Indian war arrow flints). It is quite pronounced, the deepest part being near the river. The variations of the tee-shot from the diagonally placed teeing ground are quite obvious.

The hole illustrated by Figure Two is interesting, I think, for the green is constructed near a point where the river and the Binniekill meet. The hole is a mashie length

from a very wide teeing ground on the bluff looking down on nothing but a green and a causeway leading down to it. The surroundings are particularly beautiful, although the water hazard figures in no other way than in the event of an unusual overplay.

But at this comparatively low point the green itself has been built up in an imposing manner with river stones as a foundation. Of course these have been covered with soil and present entirely natural slopes. A glance at the sketch will reveal an infinite variety of play from the teeing ground.

In constructing these holes, and all others at Poxono, I made no effort to construct previously conceived holes but in every instance permitted the general terrain and outstanding natural features to suggest the proper type. It is my opinion that this method should be pursued by the golf architect in all instances.

The third hole at Shawnee with a glimpse of the Delaware in the background.

37 BUILDING ELASTICITY

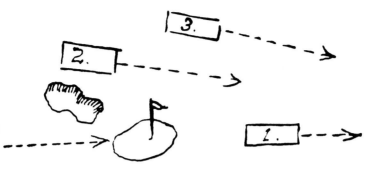

A PLAIN LITTLE sketch may be worthy of a place upon this page. The drawing is intended to provide a construction "Don't." A putting green is shown with the next teeing ground placed directly behind it. This fault is not encountered frequently on courses of the highest class but often upon those built in the days when the golf architect did not keep in mind so many details as now.

In these days of long flying balls we are forced to insure the future values of the various holes against even more lively balls than those of the present. A few years since, a course which measured up to six thousand yards was regarded as a thoroughly satisfactory, championship test. Now we are creeping up to sixty-five and sixty-six hundred yard totals from the back teeing grounds, with the average daily play several hundred yards less. Holes of four hundred and twenty-five yards once were regarded as long two-shotters. Today we are adding fifty yards to this length because of the constant introduction of longer flying balls. So, let us back to the sketch for a moment.

In the case of teeing ground, marked 1, there can be no lengthening of the hole from that end, but by building on the side, as in the cases of 2 and 3, the hole may be lengthened without serious inconvenience. We must endeavor to make our modern courses as elastic as possible, and when we are forced to lengthen out it is far more economical to build new teeing grounds and hazards than to construct new putting greens.

A consultation with the foreman as to topographical details when the architect explains his ideas for the work under construction.

NOT long since I heard several spirited discussions between players and green committeemen. The subject was the same in both instances, the merits or possible defects of certain holes which were referred to as "Blind."

Probably holes of the same kind are responsible for more arguments than any others and considerable might be written about them.

In both instances the greens could not be seen from the teeing grounds, but long and accurately placed drives will enable the player to see them plainly for his second, about a mashie in both cases. One of the holes is the Alps at Lido and the other is the Island at Shackamaxon. In playing the Alps a very pronounced hillock shuts off the view of the green. The approach to the green is blind excepting when the drive has been placed well over on the right of the fairway, and a long one, too. The left side is easier to play to, and one has to court considerable trouble in playing over to the right.

In playing the Island hole at Shackamaxon, a tee shot of about 240 yards enables the player to look down upon the patch of green in the lake, and by the way this green needs raising in the back. It is much too formal now. In commenting upon this hole it was referred to as "Blind," but I insist that it is not. Certainly it is from parts of the fairway where the short drives come to rest, but there is no reason why the man who drives so short should have a less difficult shot than he who has by his own efforts removed the blindness.

Any hole which must keep its green concealed from all parts of the fairway is open to severe criticism. The fault is less objectionable if the shot is a very long one, and cer-

The ninth at Shackamaxon. Not content with surrounding the hole with water and trees, the architect added a unique hazard touch by placing a rough grass mound on this green, an "island" on the island. The entrance is to the left side of the sketch.

tainly no short hole should be so constructed as to hide the real objective, the cup itself, from the sight of the player. I refer to greens which take a pitch from the teeing ground. But just because a short hitter may be placed in the position of taking his mashie and playing blindly to a green, after the drive, does not make it a blind hole by any means.

On nearly every course there is a blind, or partially blind, hole or two. You will find these the most heartily abused of any. But be sure they are blind before changing them.

No hole may be condemned as blind if it is so because the feeble hitting of the player makes it so. Some of the best holes are great because visibility of the green is only gained because a fine shot opens it to sight.

Recently I was asked to express an opinion concerning a green which was half-blind to a mashie pitch from the teeing-ground. The stand that I take on this question is most decided. Such a green should allow the player to see his pitch strike on the green and to observe its every hop or twist. This applies to any green which should be reached by a lofted iron either from teeing-ground or fairway. There are some truly excellent holes whose greens are half-blind to long shots, and an absolutely blind drive at times is no objection so long the objective is not a green. Often there are blind shots to greens when the preceding shots have not been hit far enough or placed with sufficient accuracy to open up the flag to full sight. Certainly this goes a long way to the making of a good hole. But a blind approach from teeing-ground to green or from fairway after the drive has been played to the queen's taste? Never!

Even though the water surrounds the ninth green of the Shackamaxon Country Club in New Jersey, and has collected as tribute its full share of golf balls, it is still considered one of the most charming water holes in the country, even by those who have been penalized by its presence. More pictures have been taken of this hole than any other of similar character, outside of the fifth at Pine Valley. The growing water lilies and reflecting shadows make it constantly attractive. It is the usual gathering place of galleries at club, invitation, State or other tournaments.

39   THE REDAN HOLE

A most beautiful Redan at Somerset Hills.

SOME of the most interesting holes are those where the best line of the flag is not direct. As has been pointed out already, the modern putting green is not a symmetrical affair showing about the same face from either side, but a rugged creation, usually constructed artificially to resemble nature as closely as possible, and from the left hand side of the fairway the appearance of such a green is quite different from its appearance from the right.

Every player who does something more than slog a ball, who thinks as he plays, appreciates why greens are built in this manner. He knows that by placing successfully his shots on one side of the fairway his next shot to the green will be more easily managed. Now the immediate approach to a green receives quite as much care in construction as does the green itself. The architect plans that a ball finding the green from the right, let us say, shall receive considerable assistance in getting home, provided it has been skillfully placed. Pronounced undulations are introduced for this purpose and from these a ball will kick in safely if properly played, or else be deflected considerably if slightly off-line. Therefore the correct line of play is not always straight on the pin.

The Redan hole at North Berwick offers a striking example of the feature referred to. This famous hole has been copied frequently on American courses, and some of the efforts have resulted in very good holes, too, even though they may differ considerably from the original. But the entrance to the Redan green is from the right and the green slopes considerably on the extreme left. "Falls away" better expresses it.

A prominent mound appears at this entrance and if the ball finds it nicely it will kick in, but if it gets working too far to the right it is a case of "helangone" as the caddie would say.

The player finds a prominent mound in the left center of the green, which is half eaten into by a great sand pit on the front and right. As a result of this mound the character of the approach to this green depends entirely upon the position of the cup and considerable variety is furnished. From the mound a properly placed ball will be thrown in for a run to the cup. When the hole is cut in the extreme left rear corner the shot is very different and considerably more difficult.

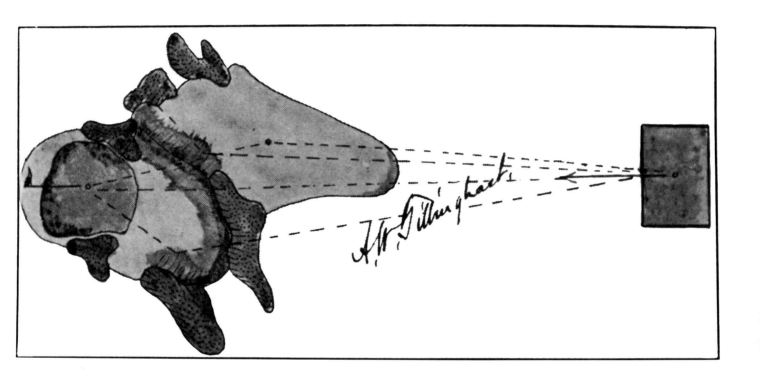

IT IS GENERALLY CONCEDED that any course must stand or fall by reason of the character of its one-shot holes. Not that the others may be weak and the one-shotters alone claim distinction, but certainly uninspiring par threes will never lift an otherwise fine course above mediocrity. It is the thought of some that the one-shot hole needs only to provide a teeing-ground and a green with immediately surrounding hazards. But as a matter of fact the approach is of incalculable value when constructed to lend finesse to the play.

My sketch generally describes a length of approximately two hundred and twenty-five yards (or with this playing length under normal conditions). A similar hole was originated by me at Newport, and variations to suit conditions have been constructed on other courses with gratifying results.

The outstanding feature of the type, is provided by a ridge, graded naturally in diagonal meandering across the fairway, dividing it into distinct areas. The way to the green on the left is only for the courageous with a long carry directly over the large pit. On the right, the less ambitious may find a comfortable route well satisfied if a careful 4 goes on the card.

Four tee shots are indicated by the dotted lines. Two are quite obvious, I think—the raking shot home and the careful two-to-the-green on the right. Another shows the deflection into a pit from a long, off-line shot on the right. The other may need a bit of scrutiny for it represents a kick to the green from a slightly pulled shot into the throw on the extreme left of the fairway, a dangerous chance, however, if the distance is not gauged nicely, for pits fore and aft wait for erring.

This hole places a premium on accurate placement from the tee, with interesting grading of play. I named the type "The Reef" because of the diagonal spine which suggested treacherous reef water outside the harbor.

41 THE THREE SHOTTER

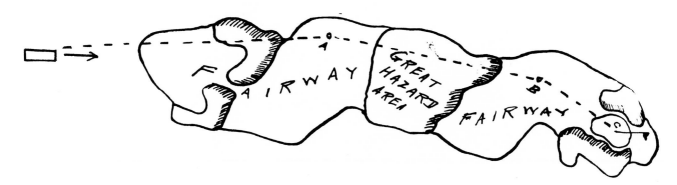

FOR THE MOST PART the three-shotters which are encountered on the average courses are nondescripts beyond the range of two shots. Frequently they are of great length, 600 yards or more, and requiring only three stout strokes with wood to reach the green. Certainly there is no great satisfaction in blazing away on such a hole, so utterly lacking in features which require finesse and accurate play. There must be something along the line which makes one think, something to invite brave endeavor and a suitable reward for the accomplishment. Not only must there be something, but many things, for the real three-shotter must be bunkered with all the careful consideration and nice care of any short hole, which must rely upon its hazards to make it notable. The ideal three-shot hole is a combination of a long two-shotter and a short one—two long shots so played as to permit the next, an accurate iron, to find and hold the green. I believe that only a hole such as this may be regarded as a satisfactory three-shotter. One of the most respected golf architects in America differs with me in the estimate of holes of this type. I recall a friendly argument, and I have no hesitation in presenting his views. He insists that such a hole should present a green of generous dimensions, one sufficiently large to receive a very long shot, and that the hole should always be open to two prodigious shots if the player can bring them off.

To this argument I take decided exception. In the first place our putting greens must be built with the shot which is to find them in mind. The size of the greens, their very contour must fit the shot. How, then, can we conceive and construct that most vital feature if we admit that shots of one kind are to reach home ordinarily, and on unusual occasions an entirely different stroke is to do it? In brief, I hold that a three-shot hole must call for three shots from any man, and never two abnormal ones. Else, how is it a three-shot hole?

If the green is to be open to two shots, the whole scheme of hazards must be entirely different from any conceived to guard against a third stroke which is short and placed with great precision. A man cannot serve two masters, nor can a golf hole be satisfactory if two shots, so very different as is the full brassey and a pitch from mid-iron or mashie, be considered when the green and its approaches are designed and built.

In my humble opinion the green to the three-shot hole

Baltusrol's "Sahara" on the seventeenth of the Lower Course.

must be beyond the range of any player who misses either his drive or second stroke. Dog-legging enables us to accomplish this. But the most effectual method, and I believe the only satisfactory one, is the location of a truly formidable hazard across the fairway. This must be carried with the second shot if the green is to be gained with the third. Obviously this break in the fairway must be great, let us say 100 yards, for it not only has to be crossed with the second, but also keep any shot short of it from getting home. Assuming that the green has been closely bunkered and of no great proportions, it is unlikely that a very long shot would hold under any conditions, but the big break prevents any half topped second from getting within range of the green and it offers a respectable carry for any well-hit second which is to follow a good drive.

Refer to the rough sketch, and in it there will be found the idea of the three-shot hole in which the great hazard area is a prime factor. Let us assume that this rough area be of sand, if the locality makes it possible, or of any sort of rough which the region affords. It measures about 100 yards across and the far brink is 400 yards from the teeing ground. A hole such as this should be provided with at least three teeing grounds, and, of course, the weather conditions must dictate which one is to be used. With the following wind, when the hole might be stretched to its extreme length, the carry for the second would be even greater than the yardage given above; with a head wind it would be considerably less. but the vital point to be remembered is this: that big break across the fairway is to present a fair but fine carry for any second shot which is to open up the green to the third, and at the same time stop anything which has not been well played from getting to the green at all.

The three shot fourteenth at Quaker Ridge.

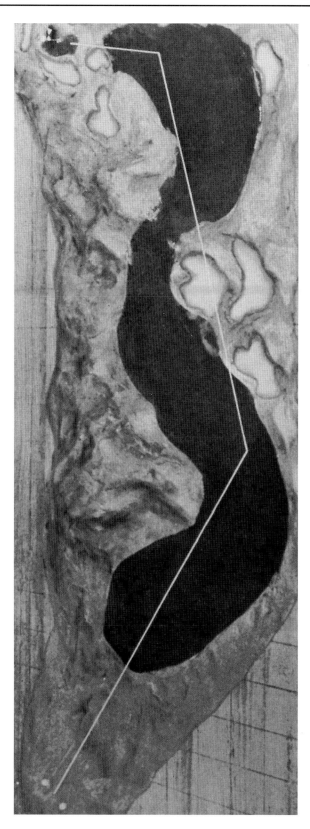

COMPARATIVELY speaking there are more thoroughly bad three-shot holes than those of any other type. In most instances they have been conceived with the thought of brawn rather than finesse. With three shots in mind, very frequently the designers of holes have considered length alone, ignoring the relation which each stroke should bear to the others.

The ideal three-shotter demands a long well-placed drive followed by an equally controlled brassey or cleek to a point from which a small closely-guarded green presents its most attractive face to an accurate approach.

Obviously it is necessary to construct the hole in a fashion which will place the green beyond the range of a third shot if either the drive or the second has been badly hit. An effective way of accomplishing this is by breaking the fairway by an immense area of hazard or rough, which must be carried by the second before the green is within range and of sufficient width to prevent the player getting home if his ball is short of it. A fine example of this type is provided by the seventh hole at Pine Valley, where the sand hazard is in the neighborhood of one hundred yards across. The seventh at Garden City presents a section of rough country directly across its fairway.

I have modeled a three-shot hole of an entirely new type, and inasmuch as the perspective of the photograph is likely to be a bit misleading, possibly a few words of explanation will be not amiss. The three-shotter illustrated by my model shows a double dog-leg twisting around the right of hillocks which in this instance were covered by trees. The broken area along the left is of such rough character that any shot over it cannot be considered and inasmuch as the putting green is bunkered severely on the left, it only can be approached with any degree of safety from the fairway around the second bend.

A hole of this description was constructed afterwards at St. Albans, but there the corners of woods extended in from the right. In the sketch we present we have a variation of the Double Dog-Legged three-shotter. It will be noticed that the encroachments appear alternatively for the left and right, and even greater variety is provided. In the selection of a plan for the double bend it will be necessary, of course, to determine which is best suited to existing conditions.

Let us briefly analyze the sketch. From the teeing grounds an elbow of trees makes into the fairway from the left and the tee-shot must be sufficiently long to reach beyond this if the second, equally well hit, is to open up the green, which nestles away beyond the second elbow, extending in from the other side of the fairway. The arrangement of pits precludes the possibility of half-topped shots gaining points of advantage, and the green demands a lofted approach. To be thoroughly sound, a three shot hole must call for two long, well-placed shots from play clubs and then a controlled approach.

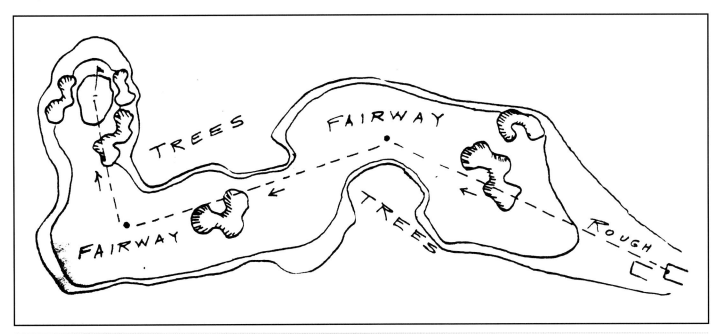

"Hell's Half Acre" on the seventh hole at Pine Valley, bisects the fairway providing a great three shotter.

43 A PRACTICAL PRACTICE GROUND

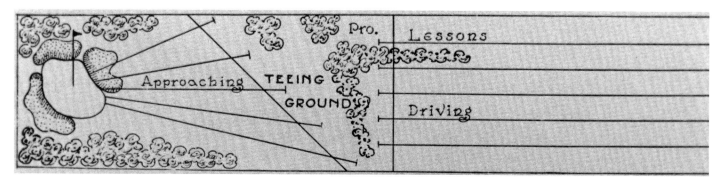

GROUND for Practice in proximity to the club-house is one of the essentials of the modern golf course. The need of it is recognized generally and demanded. The question of how to plan such an area to be given over for the practicing of various shots to as many as possible at one time is one which this article will attempt to answer.

When courses were planned in this country years ago, little heed was given as a rule to any practice ground. The pro was forced to get a toe-hold on any little patch near his club-shop and this pawky corner quickly became denuded of turf and his pupils were forced to knock their shots from a worn, clay surface rather than learn to nip them properly from turf. The instructor knew that this was wrong and the plea for suitable grounds for instruction and practice first came from the professionals. I think that nowhere will be found any who takes a more genuine interest in the progress of his pupils than the golf pro, and this honest desire prompted the request, which unfortunately was given but scant attention until the players themselves realized that the practicing of their strokes from well-kept turf was improving their games. It may not be far from fact to say that the excellence of American golf found itself with the recognition of the necessity of suitable practice grounds.

Today, committees, who are entrusted with the building of new courses or the reconstruction of old ones, invariably stress this point in conferences with the course architect. Indeed the realization of its importance is such that in instances where the lack of space around the clubhouse will not permit of that greatly desired plan of two swings of nine holes and practice ground, too—the former arrangement is abandoned frequently and the practice

ground given preference. But this should not be necessary if sufficient study is given to the selection of the site for the clubhouse. There should be room for both features, and it is possible that the sketch on this page may help.

It is to be inferred that at another nearby spot there exists a practice putting green such as will be found near every clubhouse, and it is to be hoped that this offers true turf. The plan which is illustrated provides for every shot in the bag, explosion and deft pitches from sand pits included, but it is best that the green be used only for approaches from the varying lengths. I am pleased to call this plan The Ridgewood, for it was there that it was originated when the new courses in North Jersey were planned. Let us regard it for a moment.

The Green itself was contoured and turfed exactly as any other of the twenty-seven, and the entire area maintained quite as carefully—teeing grounds, fairway and sand pits. It will be noted that the contour of the green shows the proper face to all approaches, which grade in length from a mashie-niblick to an iron of 175 yards. The teeing ground is immense, not only for the purpose of providing varying lengths for a number of players at one time but also to allow repairs to wear and tear. Immediately back of those who practice with irons to the green, there is a planting of trees and shrubbery, which completely isolates the play directly on the other side. From this side of the teeing ground, certainly seven or eight may drive simultaneously and without crowding (although the sketch shows but four lines). The range of the drives is up to nearly three hundred yards.

Now for the feature which I fancy—the private corner, completely screened by tree and shrubbery planting, for the instructor and his pupil. Naturally enough every one, seeking instruction and coaching, would prefer to concentrate, giving ear to the pro without the irritating presence of observers. Such distractions cannot help and it would be equally annoying to consult a physician with all the other patients grouped around wagging their heads knowingly and in pity. I have observed novices at their golf lessons, getting along famously under the soothing encouragement of the instructor, suddenly tighten up and begin to hash horribly because of the embarrassing intrusion of an onlooker. It seems to me that this plan has merit, and I know it works out well, for after building the first one at Ridgewood, I introduced similar arrangements at other courses and without exception they are most satisfactory. Truly it is *Multum in parvo*.

As an illustration of the handicap of inadequate instruction grounds, I will refer to Elmsford in Westchester. (And I know that the gentlemen of that club will not mind inasmuch as that course is undergoing a complete reconstruction.) Until now the Turnesa boys have been forced to instruct their pupils directly in open fairways and in the face of constant play. Under these conditions, none of the instructors or pupils could give undivided attention to the lessons even during the hours when play over the course was desultory, and at times when the procession was regular the instruction and practice had to cease. Throughout the country there are many similar conditions, though happily not so frequently encountered as formerly. On course after course are to be observed solitary players tearing up the fairway within a small area with divots all about as they practice to the serious damage to the regular course and great danger to themselves and others. And I am not the Pharisee as I regard these evils for in the past I have sinned when I have not stood firmly for adequate practice space when there was none too much property. But there came a time when a great light came over me and I resolved to sin no more. The finding of a practice ground is essential—near the clubhouse if possible but somewhere without a doubt, even in a remote corner. It is not the most desirable thing for the pro to have to walk far from his shop with his pupil or for the fellow who has a half hour or so to keep in stroke to have to waste good time in getting there and back, but even so, it is better than being forced to massacre the regular course.

Ridgewood Site Plan with practice range indicated on upper left.

44

The Ninth At Fresh Meadow: Looking across the gully between the tee and the green. The hole is 143 yards to a small closely-bunkered green. The short excellent holes at Fresh Meadow all call for accurate play, though they are not excessively difficult. Fresh Meadow is a very well designed course whereas a low score must be thoroughly earned by good work. The secret of Fresh Meadow is no secret at all, long accurate second shots after long placed drives. It was the same principle at Baltusrol in the 1926 championship and at Winged Foot in 1929.

JUST why the fact that one or several players succeeded in getting around any course in the 60's in the major championships, should be regarded as a reflection on the demands of the course, is difficult for me to appreciate. But, undoubtedly, there are many who regard such performances as calamities. These are confined to the members of the club, whose course has been thus humiliated (as they think) and more particularly the mem-

bers of the green committees who have groomed their course for the big shows of golf. Such reaction to inspired, sub-par scoring is foolish. *There is no course in the world that will prevent the right player from breaking 70 if it is his day to get all the breaks of the game.*

The comparison of scores over various courses through successive years may be indicative of the merits of the holes as judged by their measure to true championship test, and then again it may not. Weather conditions are the chief factor in throwing out of gear any system of calculating comparative scores as a basis of comparative merit. Then, too, it is not beyond the bounds of imagination to conceive of a collection of holes that contains enough bad ones as to discount the excellence of play; freakish holes that stubbornly resist the best of shots and turn them to disaster. And this thought rather suggests the observation that high scoring is not always proof that a course may be altogether an admirable test of fine shots, neither does a score (or scores) in the 60's by any means indicate that the holes, individually and collectively, are wanting in testing qualities. Indeed, I am inclined to believe that a very fine shot-maker in a scoring mood will be more likely to make a very low score over a very exacting course, where contours of fairway and greens adequately reward and punish, than over an easier route where greens may not be trusted to hold courageous play at all times. However, it is a fair assumption that the summary of scores which reveals figures in the 60's as a not uncommon round among the leaders, represents play over a rather ordinary lay-out. So, after all, it may be said truly that under normal conditions we do not like to see too many cards turned in that show that par has been bettered by four or five strokes. We do not express our admiration of the few at all grudgingly, but if the consistent beating of par seems to be getting a habit with the field, we surely turn our thoughts to the strengthening of our defenses.

My own observations in checking the play over such courses of mine as have been the scenes of National and Sectional championships, have made me firmly convinced that the character of the one-shot or par 3 holes has more to do in checking the assaults of the 70 breakers than any other factor. For example, let us assume that a certain course possesses the usual number of one-shot holes—four or perhaps only three. If these four one-shotters are mediocre or so wide open as to make the shot from the tee a not particularly testing effort, and probably providing no

The 293rd shot of Bobby Jones at the Open. The ball lay on the edge of a bunker of the eighteenth green. This shot was chipped within 12 feet of the hole. A 12-foot putt tied Al Espinosa and made 35 golf writers that expected to snooze on Sunday turn out at 9:30 A.M. and work all day covering the 36-hole play-off. If that putt had been missed, Chicago would have greeted Al Espinosa with a band and fireworks.

great punishment if the green is not gained or held—these easy par 3 holes only seem to be great opportunities for the cracks to record birdie 2's, and they look for probable 3's by reason of deadly chip shots or pitches, even though the green has been missed entirely. Such holes may be scenically beautiful and inspiring enough ordinarily, but if they do not show teeth which will bite and hurt they are rather held in contempt by the cracks in the classics, and shots, even from the tournament teeing grounds, that are not exacting enough to make it necessary to take unusual pains are unworthy. The short holes on championship courses should be the most feared of any, and any player who cracks 70 should face fear and conquer it if his performance is to be rated a truly great one. I recall that Bobby Jones, during the practice rounds at Winged Foot prior to the Open Championship there, asserted that he would be well satisfied to score par each time on the one shotters of this course. As a matter of fact birdies on the four short holes at Winged Foot during that Open were comparatively few and 4's were plentiful, simply because these holes were commanding of respect. As I recall 70 was broken there by only one man, Jones. I have a score card which I have kept since the 23rd of July, 1897. It records a round made by Willie Auchterlonie over the Old Course at St. Andrews, Scotland, on that date:

Out 4 5 4 3 3 5 4 4 4—36
In   4 2 4 4 4 4 4 5 4—35—71

Although I visited St. Andrews on numerous occasions after that date, and until the rubber cored ball came into play in 1901, I do not recall a better score there with the old gutta percha ball, which, as old-timers can tell you, took a lot of hitting. Certainly this performance today with modern balls and clubs would rate with the 65's and 66's, for the par at St. Andrews in those days was 76. This round of Auchterlonie's beat the best previous rounds of 72, made by Andrew Kirkaldy in 1895 and by that great amateur, Fred Tait, in 1894. These rounds, breaking par by four and five strokes, would score in the 60's today as stated before, but I never heard anyone suggest that the classic green of Old St. Andrews was a "push-over" and gone to the bow-wows generally, simply because several of the world's best golfers happened to be in a scoring mood on days when they got the breaks. At that they might have done better, for on the home hole, Tait took a 4, Kirkaldy a 5, and Auchterlonie a 4, which was par. This home hole measured around 375 or 380 yards as I recall it, and on one occasion it was over-driven by that mighty hitter, Blackwell, and he did it with a "gutty" ball.

To avoid the imagined disgrace of having 70 broken in the tournaments, the committees sometimes (only to frequently as a matter of fact) cut the holes on the greens in hazardous and tricky parts. A good course certainly requires no such treatment. However, there is meat enough in this for a subsequent article. The real thought of this one may be summed up in the remark that any great course will now and then take a good beating from good men, and there is nothing that can be done fairly to stop it, nor any reason why there should.

Quaker Ridge Golf Club where the Metropolitan Amateur was held in 1932.

45

THE FETISH OF LENGTH

The seventh hole at Knollwood rolls downhill from a slightly elevated tee.

WE REGARD the present tendency to stretch golf courses out to greater lengths than ever before, as an unfortunate and mistaken policy. To make our courses generally more enjoyable to the great majority, we rather incline to the conviction that *shorter holes* and *smaller greens* would be much better. The average golfer, who cannot begin to get the prodigious lengths of the mighty ones, *does* like to encounter holes that are not beyond the range of two of his best efforts. When he is forced to face the necessity of covering four hundred and sixty yards to accomplish this under normal conditions, he can't quite make it with any two shots in his bag. Yet a hole of this length and longer is plain duck soup to the great players with but few exceptions.

Certainly such holes must be provided for occasions when the big fellows are competing, but for the day-in and day-out play of the modest ones, who yet delight in calling themselves "golfers," considerably less length should be offered. Of course, this highly desirable situation may be provided by having very long teeing grounds, or even auxiliary ones, which will permit of the placement of the markers out toward the fronts. Undoubtedly this is the solution. But when the shorter ranges are not considered, or not possible because the teeing areas are restricted and insignificant, then the situation is deplorable. However, after looking over a number of the most recently constructed courses, we come flatly back to the observation of our opening paragraph. Why, it is actually a fact that we have encountered the effort to produce "the longest hole in the world." The merit of any hole is not judged by its length but rather by its interest and its variety as elective play is apparent. It isn't *how far* but *how good*!

But the fetish of distance is worshipped entirely too often and there should be a quick end to it. Very recently, in California during one of the open tournaments, we heard a noted player asked his opinion of the course. "It's too damned long!" came the instant and candid reply—and this answer was made by one of the longest hitters in our land. And with this note of confidence from one for whom long holes have no terrors, we are for the present content to rest our case.

A NEWLY-APPOINTED chairman of a green committee has written me a letter, asking an opinion of the duties of the position so far as its relationship with subordinates is concerned.

To my way of thinking, after connections with many green committees in all sections of the country, the fewer subordinates the better. A committee of three or five is quite large enough. A greater number is likely to prove unwieldy and generally includes considerable dead wood. Anyone, who is not willing to devote a fair amount of time to committee work, should not be considered as worthy of a place on a committee, which is of such great importance. Of course there are cases where a man is placed among the keepers of the course solely for the benefit of his knowledge and experience, even though the time he is enabled to give is limited. But generally speaking, the green committeeman must be useful and not ornamental, a man willing to follow the policies of the chairman to the letter.

The "chief" should be a dictator, for the green committee is a one-man show if there ever was one. The chairman should be a man of considerable knowledge of turf conditions and the requirements of the game itself. It is to be assumed that these qualifications have caused his selection. Then everything should be left entirely to his judgment. He should be permitted to select his associates, and not forced to accept appointments, which almost invariably are not entirely to his liking. There must be no opportunity for anyone to drop a monkey-wrench in the machinery.

It is unfortunate if the chairman happens to be narrow-minded. He will get better results by listening to any scrap of information even though he does not accept it as good. He should welcome criticism and seek knowledge from those who have had experience. He should be tactful and give ear to the suggestions of even the humblest duffer. Certainly he will get many an earful of drivel and senseless complaint, but it is a portion of his job. Yet, often enough the criticisms are just and valuable. He must not feel hurt if he does not receive words of general encouragement and praise, which in his heart he knows he merits. The average player is not over-given to plaudits, but trust him to roar if he has a grievance either real or fancied. The reward of the chairman is his own satisfaction in doing his work well. He must have the courage of his convictions and stick tenaciously to a policy when he has determined that it is right.

The author, with Chandler Egan(l), and Jack Neville looking over the links at Pebble Beach during the 1929 Amateur.

In answering the query of our correspondent I urge him to outline his course of action to his subordinates, clearly defining the work that each man must do, and above all—gently but firmly break the news that the chairman is boss, and that he intends to continue in that capacity. In case of mutiny during the cruise, make the culprit walk the plank without delay. When doctors disagree, the patient dies. No course can thrive under various experiments, caused by the differing opinions of a divided committee. The green committee must depend upon the singleness of one man's purpose. His associates must assist, but in no sense oppose. And after the chairman's term has ended, his policies should be carried on by his successor. The surest way to ruin a course is by an ever-changing policy. "A new broom sweeps clean." This old adage never applied more fitly to anything so well as the assuming of one man's job by another. But it spells disaster in the case of green committees, excepting when the retiring members have proven rank failures.

47 EVER CHANGING POLICIES

ON SEVERAL OCCASIONS I have referred to the evils of an ever-changing policy of course upkeep. Nothing can result so disastrously to the turf or cause greater demands on the club treasuries. It seems timely to discuss the subject more thoroughly.

In many clubs the selection of a green committee is accomplished with little more concern than would attend the purchase of a household doormat; something necessary and fairly durable and which, when worn out, may be tossed aside for a new one. Often the chairman of the committee is decided on because he has enough spare time to visit the course frequently and observe the work of the laborers, and this he does conscientiously but often ignorantly. Sometimes the chairman considers that he has performed his duties thoroughly if his force keeps the grass cut regularly, the rough and hazards trim and clean, and the accessories of up-keep in good condition. I recall one gentleman who was so diligent in the cutting of the fairway that he always kept the grass closely cropped for a considerable space *behind* the teeing grounds.

When a willing chairman has been selected, he often has as assistants a half dozen or more gentleman, some quite as willing as himself to devote considerable time to observation and others who devote their entire time to kicking. Other clubs are more fortunate in selecting a green committee chairman, who makes a close study of the turf conditions and who proceeds along well-defined lines. At first he may have no great knowledge of soils or of the peculiar treatment of golf turf. It is likely that he does know something of drainage. But he has to learn by keen observation and through consultations with experienced men, and, which is most important of all, by reason of his own experiments. For example, he soon must be convinced that a truly turfed putting green cannot be maintained by rolling out irregularities. At first he probably jumped at the conclusion that a good heavy rolling after showers or watering must be the surest way to produce a smooth putting surface. By experience, sad and costly, he must find that this is the surest way of ruining what little turf he already may have developed. The successful green committeeman must be observing and thirsty for knowledge. He must have a retentive memory or be methodical in his recording of data. He must be open-minded and willing to lend ear to advice, which may exactly oppose his deep-rooted theories. He must be willing to experiment patiently in order to accept and discard suggestions. But he must have time to enable any line of treatment to work out its salvation.

It is because the policies of green committees are changed so often that wholly satisfying turf conditions are encountered so rarely. It will be noted that I say "policies." Simply because the head of the committee is relieved of his duties is no reason why there should be any deviation from an established policy of his which may be proving its worth. While the chairman may be sort of a dictator, he will, if he be a man of sense, thoroughly discuss his plans with his fellow committeemen. And let me digress to say that I believe a committee of five to be quite large enough, while, as a matter of fact, three are better. That the committee be in general accord with the policy of the chairman is essential. Each member should be thoroughly familiar with every detail of proposed bunkering and the treatment of the turf, and when the new chairman takes the place of the old he should be selected from the committee in order that there may be no radical change in that methodical plugging away along one line which must bring results if it is sound.

It must be remembered that there are several paths to success. There may be more than one way of getting the best of some troublesome local condition, and any one of them may be excellent so long as it is backed by perseverance. But a compromise is likely to accomplish nothing. I recall the excellent putting greens of one of America's most noted courses. The policy of selecting none but a member of the previous green committee to serve as a new chairman has been followed for years. Nearly without exception the excellence of turf on our leading courses may be traced to one unvarying policy. To be sure, there have been times when experts have been called in to investigate an unusual condition, but the treatment of petty ills has interfered in no great measure from the old steady, wholesome diet.

Among the small organizations particularly there exists the tendency to clean house every year or two. Probably the chairman of the green committee has found his duties a bit irksome. After starting in with all the enthusiasm imaginable he finds the novelty wearing away after a while. In every club there are chronic kickers. They object to the placement of certain hazards; the condition of the putting greens never satisfies them; they constantly demand the rolling of the greens; the rough is always too rank, etc. It takes a level-headed chairman to listen to every objection and be tactfully firm at all times. He must have a hide like a rhinoceros to turn aside all the kicks which are let fly at him. But to be successful he must adhere unwaveringly to the course which he has convinced himself to be right. But so often he tosses up the sponge and steps aside. Probably one of the very men who have opposed his policies most strenuously is selected as his successor. What happens? The new chairman blindly rushes to a complete change of everything. Old pits are filled and new ones digged without any thought of a pre-conceived scheme of hazards, until the poor course resembles a crazy quilt. Under the old treatment, the turf may be starting in the proper way to quality. The new committee decides over night on a drastic change and in a few weeks the work of several years is destroyed. And so it goes. Every year or two there is a revolution and a new regime is declared. Every one pulls against the other, but in the meanwhile the course goes to the bow-wows.

Sheep keep the new Suneagles fairways trim. Seymour Dunn, in kilts and Daughter Doris play a round.

Rocks are not impassible obstacles in the construction of fairways, as the work at the Scarsdale club shows.

48

THE KILKENNY CATS

WHENEVER the green committee attempts improvements and reconstruction work, there is sure to be launched a certain amount of criticism. This fault-finding is bound to crop out, no matter how sound and excellent the work may be. As a rule the carpers are in hopeless minority but they make a lot of noise for this very reason. The players, who are blessed with common sense, patiently wait until they have played over the changed conditions, then critically, but fairly, attempt an analysis. It has been said that a block-head can find more fault with a course than a wise constructor could ever accomplish. Frankly it is best to regard the chronic objectors as block-heads and treat them with all possible toleration. Certainly every committee is firmly convinced that their particular club includes more fault-finders than any other, but they are to be encountered everywhere and it is likely that they are distributed about rather evenly. What a blessing it would be if it were only possible to concentrate them all in one organization, and give them free rein. What a course they would have! What debates and wrangles! The Kilkenny cats would lose their renown.

Not long ago some recent construction work was abused loud and long. It assumed the aspects of a tempest, but after getting down to the bottom of the situation, the committee discovered that the criticisms were those of exactly three members. It was not long before the storm subsided, for the players, on the whole, welcomed the improvements and appreciated them.

The sixteenth green of the "Binnikill" hole at Shawnee.

BEFORE the dawn of the present century there were not so many golf courses spread over our country as compared with the present, but still there were a goodly number. Each club had its green committee, of course, or greens committee as they erroneously were called (and frequently still are). Taking these committees by and large, and regarding them through our spectacles of today, it can only be said that one was dumber than another. There were a few exceptions.

But at that remote period, few comprehended any difference between golf turf and just grass, and it was the com-

In breaking ground for a course in the old days, they had to depend solely on Dobbin and his mate to drag plows and harrows. This pictures the beginning of Fox Hills on Staten Island.

mon practice, each spring, to start work on nearly every golf course to prepare it for play, in a thoroughly conventional manner. The method was somewhat as follows: When the chairman could walk over the course without "ditching his dogs," or, in other words, getting his feet too muddy, he immediately raised a plaintive wail for the immediate attendance of the grounds-man (this was before the day of real greenkeepers).

"Ambrose, it's time for the steam roller," the C. of the G. C. would announce, definitely and impressively. "Go and see Clancy."

Now this object of the quest of Ambrose would be a conveniently located road contractor, who owned a steam

roller weighing between ten and twenty tons. After the annual dickering for the best terms for the hire of this Juggernaut, it would be turned loose over the fairway and, believe it or not, often enough the putting greens as well, the idea being to squash everything down as flat as possible.

They would wait until enough frost had left the ground and there had been enough drying out to keep the roller

This steam roller weighed ten tons. Some were twice as ponderous. At the close of the past century it was a commom practice, albeit pernicous, to flatten golf turf with them each Spring.

from sticking fast. As the "steamer" crept along, one could see the ground *creep* ahead of the immense roller. If one also could have had ears to distinguish, and understanding to heed the protests in the language of the grass, (and I am sure there must be this quite intelligible to some knowing ones) there must have been a suspicion that all was not exactly as it should be. As a matter of fact, all was very wrong.

A *light* spring rolling can do no harm, but, harking back to the ignorance of old, the murder of turf is hard to contemplate now. Why did it take so long for men to realize that the opening of ground after the departure of winter was strictly in accordance with nature's law? Why were they so blind that they could not see that young grass plants must have air to give their roots the breath of life? Soil must be kept open if turf is to live. This truth is generally recognized today, and it is not easy to believe that there are some who still insist that heavy rolling of yielding soil is quite the sensible thing to do. Yet there are such, and when I hear them express their opinions, I mentally wish that they had to wear prickly flannel underwear just because their fathers did.

The constructor of a modern golf course, with such an abundance of improved appliances to accomplish his work, would be in utter despair if he were limited to the use of the primitive tools of the old-timers.

But while there are numerous examples of a reluctance to pull away from the customs and practices of another day, it must be borne in mind that the present generation is rather too prone to leap to things new. Not long ago I encountered a glaring illustration of this. A young graduate of evidently an ultra-modern scientific school was called in consultation to discuss the ailments of a certain golf course. The green committee had been advised by an older and experienced head to relieve a tightly compact turf condition by introducing sharp sand *into* the soil. When this advice was passed along to the young consul-

tant, he made the truly amazing retort that he did not approve of the use of sand under any condition.

Now in my experience of many years, I have never known a tight clay soil that was not improved, and improved to a tremendous extent, by the working-in of sharp sand. It is a very old practice. My first appreciation of the value of sand, incorporated with soil, dates back to 1896, when it was my good fortune to meet Old Tom Morris at St. Andrews, Scotland. For many years Tom carried on as head green-keeper there, and the excellence of the St. Andrews greens was beyond question.

"Saund, saund, laddie;" the old fellow answered emphatically when asked the prime essential for turf quality, and I have never known a green-keeper of any repute who did not recognize the great value of sharp sand. Steam roller days and their folly have gone, many obsolete methods have been replaced by new and improved ones, but there remain some truths that are just as solid today as then.

Quaker Ridge Country Club is famous for maintaining its fairways in better condition than most clubs do their putting greens. All weeds are kept out of the fairways which are maintained in perfect condition as to turf, along the lines spoken of by Dr. Monteith. Quaker Ridge is a model all may well imitate.

THE STORY OF THE GANG CUTTER

50

THE IMPROVEMENT of fairways generally throughout America during the past ten years without question may be attributed to the use of the gang mower, which makes possible frequent cutting without the constant crushing and packing of heavy rollers as was the condition formerly. It is likely that a short sketch of the introduction of the mower will be interesting, for this type in various forms is used nearly everywhere.

In 1911, after the course at Shawnee PA, had just gone through its first testing season, the late H. P. Dixon of

The first Three Gang Cutter and motive equine power

Wallingford made a visit to look over the course which I had planned the previous year. The young course had not found itself yet for the new turf was yielding unexpected lengths. The constant rolling, which went hand in hand with cutting with the mowers of that period, was packing the sandy silt soil to an alarming extent and efforts to induce manufacturers to eliminate this obvious fault were not bearing fruit. When I happened to speak of my failure in this direction to Mr. Dixon, his face lighted up and with great enthusiasm he told me of a rig which he had devised for use on his estate at Wallingford, and which he was using on the fairway of the Springhaven Country Club, of which he was chairman of the green committee.

Intensely interested, I made a visit to Wallingford and saw the mower at work at Springhaven. To be sure it was a rather crudely assembled affair consisting of three thirty-inch units (Poney cutters of standard manufacture) from

which even the wooden rollers had been removed. With reduction of the over-lap the machine cut a swath of eight-four inches and accommodated itself to undulations without scalping. It was drawn easily by one horse. Indeed it was a revelation and I made the photograph, which shows that mower, together with the first motive power which since has been supplanted to a great extent by tractors.

Hastening back to Shawnee with photographs and sketches, I enlisted the services of the village blacksmith and had castings made at a foundry in a nearby town. It may be remarked that to keep the cutters from riding, slugs of lead were introduced close to the dead-knife. Such was the first of the gang mowers of 1911.

The results were astonishing for the fairway showed an almost immediate response with healthy turf and true playing distances. The lies were fine and holes, which were laid out for drive-and-brassey length, but which had been easily within the range of a drive and jigger or mashie (owing to the packed turf condition), found their true values. When the pro's played Shawnee during the following summer they marveled at the fairway and many of them carried back to their club glowing accounts of the work of the new type of mower. And so the use of the gang cutter began its spread until the present day finds it generally used throughout America and to a large extent abroad.

COMBINATION SHAWNEE TRIPLE MOWER AND WORTHINGTON LAWN TRACTOR

WHAT THE INTRODUCTION OF THE HARVESTER AND REAPER MEANT YEARS AGO TO THE GRAIN FIELDS OF THE WORLD, THE INVENTION OF THE SHAWNEE MOWER AND WORTHINGTON TRACTOR MEANS TO THE LAWNS OF AMERICA TODAY.

IMPROVES THE TURF
DISPLACES THE HORSE
REDUCES THE EXPENSE OF CUTTING UPKEEP MORE THAN ONE-HALF

THE USE OF A TRACTOR IN COMBINATION WITH A GANG MOWER IS BROADLY COVERED BY PATENTS OWNED BY THIS COMPANY. THE PUBLIC IS WARNED AGAINST INFRINGEMENTS.

WORTHINGTON MOWER COMPANY
SUCCESSORS OF THE SHAWNEE MOWER CO.
SHAWNEE-ON-DELAWARE, PENNA.

51 MAINTAINING GREEN FAIRWAYS

DURING the past two months, the topic most generally discussed in this Metropolitan district has been the watering of fairways. Among the clubs everywhere the subject seems paramount, undoubtedly due to the drought of this summer and the naturally resultant browned condition of the turf. Those who have a sprinkling system openly brag of the fine green fairway at their club, and those who have it not have been very discontented and have been besieging their green committees with appeals, which in most instances have fallen upon deaf ears because the budgets of these times can ill afford further strain.

Undoubtedly a watering system can be installed now at less cost than would have been possible a year ago, and probably less than another year or two to come.

The eleventh at Merion Cricket Club, Philadelphia, Pa: In order to ensure perfect fairways, a complete watering system was installed especially for the Amateur Championship in 1930. The last few dry years have brought home to clubs the desirability of an efficient watering system.

It is not my purpose to exploit any system. They rate from the cheap grades of pipes, in shallow trenches, which feed through hose to movable sprinklers of various patterns, to the elaborate plan of fixed "pop-up" sprinklers which water the entire fairway with no more effort than a turn of the wrist. Certainly, I approve of them if your club has sufficient wealth to afford their installation and pay the water bills. Frequently they are necessary. Often they are not.

It is entirely superfluous to mention the vital need of an adequate water supply at every green. On every decent

course the greens have presented a proper color of healthy turf throughout the entire season. Undoubtedly necessary, too, is a system that permits the approaches to be watered nearly to the same extent as the greens. Unfortunately, this is overlooked entirely in the majority of instances. Following this argument for the presence of especially true turf in certain zones, the next thought would be directed to the particular parts of the fairway from which shots properly should be played. The zone from two hundred to three hundred yards distant from the teeing ground is next in importance. But I do not endorse the necessity of watering the entire course, or I might say the desirability, no matter how much money you may have. Surely watering may be carried to the extreme, as certainly is the case frequently in the watering of putting greens, which, investigation shows conclusively, are more readily attacked by pestilence, particularly the brown patch, when soaked too much. In many cases there is the tendency to rush to the conclusion that the fairway turf is dead after a drought because the plants are browned and seared. I do not recall in these parts ever seeing any well established fairway turf permanently destroyed by drought. Apparently dead, the grass will be restored to color when the rains do fall finally, for the roots are alive, and the man who wrote "It ain't goin' to rain no mo" took considerable liberty with facts and showed a total ignorance of the records of the weather bureau.

Recently there was a fairway watering system installed on a north Jersey course at a total cost of $15,000, and the club finds it entirely adequate and satisfactory. Over in Westchester an eighteen holes system cost double this amount and their water bill runs somewhere around a thousand dollars a month. Now the interest on $30,000 invested and the cost of water cuts quite a hole in any club's budget and it resolves itself into a question of whether an all green course during drought years is altogether worth the cost. It is to be answered by the green committees, of course, but personally I feel that a less expensive method would be completely adequate.

Naturally, it makes considerable difference when the source of the water supply is considered. If it happens that there is a natural supply from a sufficiently large lake on the property, the cost will be much less than the rates charged for water from city mains, which vary greatly. The amount of water used throughout a drought must depend to a great extent upon the judgment used as to the times of watering. For instance, if a moderate amount is introduced from time to time before the dry spell is well under way, it will not be exigent to throw huge quantities after to break through the baked crust of parched earth.

During my two visits to California, I realized the absolute necessity for complete irrigation or sprinkling of the entire fairway. During the championship at Five Farms, Chandler Egan told me that the most recent courses on the coast had clear bent fairways, which up to this time showed absolutely no evidence of brown patch. In a great country like ours, conditions vary to a vast extent and certainly entire watering of the fairways must be done in some sections. But here, there certainly does not exist this vital necessity. No drought will destroy our fairways beyond natural recovery.

From all this do not misunderstand me. It is no intention of mine to discourage fairway waterings if it may be within the limits of club budgets to afford it in a moderate way. It is a luxury, highly to be commended if you do not have to rob the budget in other more important details. The surest insurance against failing turf is the development of proper soil and enough of it for the grass to thrive in, drought or no drought. There is one course in the metropolitan district which has been browned up more than usual, and the members are calling loudly for water on the fairways. In this instance there is not enough good earth and water cannot remedy this.

An up-to-date fairway sprinkler system in action on one of the fairways of the Fresh Meadow Country Club.

52

I KNOW of one club which is about to make heroic efforts to eliminate every root of poa annua which flourishes on their greens and yet these same greens are remarkably true. This would seem to bear out the contention of one celebrated expert that poa annua should be encouraged and not despised. He asserts that if it is not regarded as a weed but nourished and kept carefully cut, it will produce wonderfully hardy and true turf. It might be well for committees to experiment a little before digging it out. If you do not know it by its scientific name, you may remember the grass with the tiny white blossoms that cover the greens in June. That is poa annua, a sort of outcast blue grass. It drops its seed plentifully and spreads rapidly. Maybe it would be well to try a test bed of it and give the poor old bum a real chance. He may prove a gentleman after all.

An experimental green at Arlington where the USGA Green Section tries out grasses. Johnny Farrell is putting against a testing machine impervious to all personal foibles and errors of form. The machine is being operated by Dr. Fred Grau.

53

THE COURSE BEAUTIFUL

Bluff Point at Lake Champlain, one of the oldest in America, is highly esteemed and regarded generally as a great test of the game. Its popularity only increases with the years.

IT SEEMS TO ME that he, who plans any hole for golf, should have two aims: first, to produce something which will provide a true test of the game, and then consider every conceivable way to make it as beautiful as possible. He should have in mind not only the skill and brawn of golfers but their eyes as well. It may be that it is the combination of a fine sense of shots and the appreciation of Nature's charm, which enables one man to climb to greater heights than can another, in whom is lacking an eye for the beautiful or perhaps an utter disregard of it in the solitary effort to build something that will test play. Certainly the playing qualities of any hole must be the first consideration, and there can be no comparison between the work of one who has adhered solely to it and that of the master of landscaping, who possesses a general idea of the requirements of modern golf. There are many truly picturesque courses which are otherwise undistinguished, and there are fine tests of golf as devoid of beauty as Mary Ellen's calico. Any real player would not speak of them in the same breath. But is it not a fact, that the great courses, those that are talked of most, combine both qualities?

It is likely that fully seventy-five per cent of golfers are keenly appreciative of the striking beauty of a picturesque hole. This estimate is conservative. But there are others who do not care a rap about their surroundings, so absorbed are they in hard play. I recall an incident of many years ago when a four-ball match came to a teeing ground, which afforded a particularly impressive view of marsh-meadow stretching away to beach and ocean. One of the players spoke of it, but his partner exclaimed: "To hell with the view; we're two down!" I wonder which was the happier in his golf?

I believe that there are a goodly number of players who find their golf a mighty good excuse to get close to nature. There are thousands of business men closing their office desks every day and turning expectantly to the links, expecting what? The breaking of a hundred? Not much! That rare feat might happen to their extreme satisfaction. It *might,* but the one thing which everyone is *sure* of is a glorious afternoon in the open with songs of birds in his ears rather than constantly tinkling bells and jangling noises; with the four walls of a room replaced by a delightful, ever-changing sight of meadow and trees and brooks, or broad stretches of ocean-sands and water. Don't think for a moment that such a man would not prefer an old-fashioned circular seat under the spreading branches of an ancient apple tree to the conventional type of teeing-ground bench, which stands out in the middle of a field, alone save for a box of sand. He probably finds as much satisfaction in the swift recollection of a barefoot boy, stealing apples from just such a tree, as in getting away one of his best drives of a hundred and fifty yards. I tell you that it is men like this, who, finding the game a rare tonic, have made it possible to build and maintain courses to such a degree of excellence that the cracks may crack the seventy's.

Fortunately our modern constructors are leaning very heavily on Nature. Every artificial formation today is made to appear as pleasing to the eye as possible. Formal mounds are giving way to creations which do not clash with their surroundings. Teeing grounds are taking on the contours of surroundings to a great extent, instead of the pawky little terraced, box-like pulpits, which seemed to shriek of wheel-barrows and spades. Instead of plunging headlong through a grove, felling and uprooting ruthlessly, some respect is being paid to fine old trees which stand out gloriously as "small-stuff" has been removed and the fairway gracefully sweeps around in dog-leg and elbow. I have in mind a line from a bit of verse, I think written by the late Joyce Kilmer—"But only God can make a tree." And I think there is nothing more beautiful to look upon than a fine tree. Yet how many great specimens have been destroyed by the builders of golf courses, who had no eye for the beautiful nor ingenuity enough to find a way to let them stand, not only to add charm to courses but actually to help the play. I plead guilty to the removal of many trees, but never have I given instructions for the destruction of a fine one without genuine regret, and then only when it was imperative. We may play around trees but certainly the only route to a hole must never be over or through them. Then, too, we must not have them directly by our putting greens for their branches deflect many erring shots to fortunate finishes, falling leaves clutter the greens and the roots sap the soil of vitality that the turf needs. But if they are not too close to the line of play, trees usually lend a fine framing for a hole, and certainly the vistas are attractive.

Some streams are unsightly when they might be made picturesque with little expense and thought. And so with many other features. On one course there stood a ruin, and the committee intended to raze it. They were persuaded to make a feature of it and with practically no cost it was made notable. But let it be understood that I do not advocate the beautifying of the course at the expense of its playing qualities. Often efforts to introduce or retain shrubbery only add to the exasperations of play. Any growth which makes the loss of balls likely should be avoided, and where the fairway finds its way through woods, the underbrush must be cleared absolutely for a considerable distance on each side. The banks of streams and lake shores should never be permitted to grow rank. Certainly the landscaping may be overdone. The effects must not be forced; which reminds me of an amusing illustration. Some years since, when constructing a certain course which I visited only occasionally because of its location, the foreman had been rather impressed by the orders to disturb no flowering shrubs until directed. He managed to get the impression that flowers were a weakness of the architect and to make a great impression he went ahead on his own initiative, transformed a slope of one of the greens, introducing a wonderfully accurate five-pointed star upon which he was preparing to plant geraniums.

Even the arrangement of sand in the hazards may be used to good advantage to beautify the course. If the pits are designed well the sand has the appearance of having been blown in rather than dumped. On seaside courses the pits usually take such an appearance naturally, but the same effect may be had inland although it stands to reason that often the difficulties of providing sand in large quantities drives the constructor to a combination with turf.

Summing it up briefly, the course beautiful adds much to the pleasure of golf without detracting in the least from its qualities as a test. Even those players who are not analytical will have strong inclinations to certain courses over others. Aside from the fact that they probably fancy the places where they have scored best, the chances are that subconsciously they have admired the scenery a bit.

The saying that "A thing of beauty is a joy forever" undoubtedly is just as much applicable to the golf course as to the most extravagantly laid out lawn or garden. Members should take great pride and encourage their groundsman in every effort he takes to keep the links in first-class condition. Invariably it is taken as a matter of course that they should be that way but how much more he would appreciate a kindly word or a little note now and then, commenting on his good work.

Rockwood Hall, on the Hudson, formerly the residence of the late William Rockefeller. The inserts show President Frank H. Hitchcock (left) and Vice President Charles Dana Gibson (right), and in the center, the club crest.

This aeroplane view gives a good idea of the property with the majestic Hudson River and Tappan Zee visible from practically every part of the two courses being laid out.

118

This work is an anthology of articles written by Albert Warren Tillinghast over twenty years between 1916 and 1936. They were orignally published in several golf magazines of the time. Our editorial contributions were the organization of the works, the collection and restoration of the photographs, and the elimination of redundancies and mundane particulars.

In putting this work together we came across a number of photographs of Tillinghast courses that we could not iden- tify—see chapters 10, 11, 25, and 26. We also learned that Tillinghast had a hand in the design or renovation of many more courses than he is cur- rently credited. These include

Rick Wolffe, Bob Trebus and Stu Wolffe

the seventh and thirteenth holes at Pine Valley and the renovation of the Virginia Country Club in Long Beach, California. If anyone can shed more light on the unknown photographs and other courses that Tillinghast touched, we would appreciate hearing from you.

The idea for this anthology grew out of our first golf book—Baltusrol 100 Years, The Centennial History of Baltusrol Golf Club. When we started our research we were aware that Tillinghast was the archi- tect of record for Baltusrol's Upper and Lower cours- es. We knew of many of his other notable courses, and we had heard many interpretations of his archi- tectural principals. But we really did not know much more than that. As Baltusrol's history took shape, we began to learn much more.

We spoke with many who knew Tillinghast, and who remembered his days designing and building Baltusrol. They recalled how he was at Baltusrol almost every day during the construction, how he was always immaculately dressed in a suit, tie and knee- high boots, and how he was often seen playing golf

with several of the members and the resident professional George Low. Evidently he was well liked by the members, and he was particularly well liked by the caddies, for he was a good player and a big tipper.

We also collected and read everything we could find by or about Tillinghast. As we read, we became smitten with Tillinghast and his genius. We were delighted to learn that he considered himself the Creator of Baltusrol and how his work at Baltusrol became his calling card, establishing him as a one of the foremost golf archi- tects in the country. But, more significantly, we became completely enamored with his writings on the golf course.

After hearing many interpretations of Tillinghast's design principals and his golf courses, and of other Tillinghast aficionados who were considering writing their own rendition on Tillinghast, we came to a sim- ple conclusion—no interpretation is necessary. Tillinghast could speak for himself! His design principals are perfectly clear and eloquently put in his writings. We therefore became convinced that when we finished Baltusrol's Centennial History we could not simply place our collection of Tillinghast treasures in an archive to wait for the writing of Baltusrol's second 100 years. The world should know of Tillinghast, his genius, and most importantly his gift to golf—The Course Beautiful.

Richard C. Wolffe, Jr.,
Robert S. Trebus
Stuart F. Wolffe
Baltusrol Golf Club
Springfield, New Jersey, 07081

CHAPTER BIBLIOGRAPHY

1. The Ideal Course, Rugged and Natural, *Golf Illustrated*, February 1935.
2. Out And In Ag'in, *Golf Illustrated*, April 1921.
3. (What Is Golf Course Architecture), Modern Golf Chats, *The Golf Course*, February 1916.
4. What Golfers Are Demanding Of The Architect, *Golf Illustrated*, August 1922.
5. Planning the Golf Course, *The Architectural Forum*, March 1925.
6. (The Home Hole), Out And In Ag'in, *Golf Illustrated*, April 1921.
7. Giving Individuality To Golf Holes, *Golf Illustrated*, January 1923; Our Green Committee Page, *Golf Illustrated*, July 1918.
8. The Clubhouse, *Golf Illustrated*, February 1921.
9. Originality In Construction, Modern Golf Chats, *The Golf Course*, June 1916.
10. Forced Construction, *Golf Illustrated*, September 1928.
11. From The Ground Up, *Golf Illustrated*, June 1928.
12. (Water Hazards), Our Green Committee Page, *Golf Illustrated*, February 1919. Our Green Committee Page, *Golf Illustrated*, December 1919.
13. Trees And The Course Beautiful, *Golf Illustrated*, March 1921.
14. (Clearing The Forest), Trees on the Course, *Golf Illustrated*, May 1932.
15. Historic Spots On Golf Courses, *Golf Illustrated*, April 1934.
16. (Twisting The Fairway), Modern Golf Chats, *The Golf Course*, April 1916; Modern Golf Chats, Twisting The Fairway, *The Golf Course*, May 1916.
17. (Deception), Our Green Committee Page, *Golf Illustrated*, May 1919.
18. Trees On The Golf Course, *Golf Illustrated*, February 1931.
19. Hill Holes, *Golf Illustrated*, March 1932.
20. The Oblique In Golf Design, *Golf Illustrated*, April 1932.
21. (Several Paths To The Green), Our Green Committee Page, *Golf Illustrated*, July 1920.
22. Featuring Putting Greens, Modern Golf Chats, *The Golf Course*, July 1916.
23. (The Cart Before The Horse), Our Green Committee Page, *Golf Illustrated*, June 1919.
24. (Contouring The Green), Golf Architecture—Greens, *Golf Illustrated*, September 1930; Our Green Committee Page, *Golf Illustrated*, May 1920; What Golfers Are Demanding Of The Architect, *Golf Illustrated*, August 1922.
25. The Gateway to the Green, *Golf Illustrated*, January 1929.
26. Reconstructing the Course, *Golf Illustrated*, July 1928.
27. (Sick Holes), Our Green Committee Page, *Golf Illustrated*, November 1919.
28. The Simplicity of Modern Bunkering, *The Professional Golfer of America*, August 1936.
29. Tucking In The Traps, *The Professional Golfer of America*, September 1936.
30. Slopes? Blend Them! *The Professional Golfer of America*, July 1936.
31. (Solid Mound Work), Modern Golf Chats, *The Golf Course*, March 1916.
32. (Duffer's Headaches), Our Green Committee Page, *Golf Illustrated*, June 1920; From the Gulf to Puget Sound, *The Professional Golfer of America*, June 1936.
33. (Introducing Sand Into The Bunker), Golf Course Design and Upkeep, *Golf Illustrated*, December 1931.
34. The Rear Guard Green, *The American Golfer*, February 1927.
35. (Teeing Grounds), New Types At Poxono, *Golf Illustrated*, November 1926; Our Green Committee Page, *Golf Illustrated*, September 1920; Our Green Committee Page, *Golf Illustrated*, November 1919.
36. New Types At Poxono, *Golf Illustrated*, November 1926.
37. (Building Elasticity), Our Green Committee Page, *Golf Illustrated*, May 1919.
38. (Blind Shots), Our Green Committee Page, *Golf Illustrated*, July 1919; Architecturally and Otherwise, *Golf Illustrated*, August 1932; Our Green Committee Page, *Golf Illustrated*, July 1920.
39. (The Redan Hole), Our Green Committee Page, *Golf Illustrated*, August 1918.
40. The Reef Hole, *The American Golfer*, December 1926.
41. (The Three-Shotter), Our Green Committee Page, *Golf Illustrated*, October 1918.
42. (The Double Dog-Leg), A Novel Type of Three-Shot Hole, *Golf Illustrated*, April 1916. Our Green Committee Page, *Golf Illustrated*, May 1918.
43. A Practical Practice Ground, *Golf Illustrated*, September 1929.
44. Judging Courses By Low Scores, *Golf Illustrated*, November 1931; Where the Open Will Be Played, *Golf Illustrated*, June 1932.
45. (The Fetish Of Length), For the Good of the Game, *Golf Illustrated*, March 1935.
46. (The Green Chariman) Our Green Committee Page, *Golf Illustrated*, September 1920.
47. (Ever Changing Policies), Our Green Committee Page, *Golf Illustrated*, March 1919.
48. (The Kilkenny Cats), Our Green Committee Page, *Golf Illustrated*, May 1918.
49. Steam Roller Days, Golf Illustrated, May 1935.
50. The Story Of The Gang Cutter, *Golfers Magazine*, April 1924.
51. Maintaining Green Fairways, *Golf Illustrated*, October 1931.
52. (Poa Annua), Our Green Committee Page, *Golf Illustrated*, July 1918.
53. (The Course Beautiful), Our Green Committee Page, *Golf Illustrated*, October 1920.